ADVANCE PRAISE FOR *FROM DIAGNOSIS TO DESTINY*

"Jacob Thompson knows about dreams not coming true. He knows about unpleasant surprises and difficult changes. He knows about bad news. Jacob has also learned a transformational lesson—that good can be seen in the bad, that hope can arrive in the sadness, that amazing opportunities await us even when obstacles have bombarded us. Jacob's words dare us to choose to endure so, we can keep on fighting.

"Open the pages of *From Diagnosis To Destiny* to learn lessons we are all craving to grasp. Read Jacob's story. Find yourself. Notice your own struggles and doubts, your weaknesses and disappointments. Don't stop there though. Notice the hope. Receive the invitations. Believe great days are ahead for Jacob and for you—for all who are willing to believe 'Your Trials Aren't Meant to Break You; They're Meant to Make You.' Whatever your diagnosis, open the pages and begin to receive direction for your destiny."

— **Chris Maxwell**
Author, Pastor, Poet

"Jacob shares his story in *From Diagnosis To Destiny*, but more importantly, he shares his hope and faith in the God Who can turn our weaknesses into great strength."

— **Bob Goff**
New York Times Best Selling Author,
Founder of LoveDoes.org

"Community is built on what we learn from observing one another. Jacob 'TEN20' Thompson is an incredible example for all of us. Through the stories of his experience living with Friedreich's Ataxia, *From Diagnosis To L* holds the spiritual and practical secrets to his success."

— **Kyle Bryant**, Athlete, A
Spokesperson for the Friedreich's Ataxia Research Alliance (

"In your hands you hold a new perspective on what it means to be fully alive. Life can throw you a curve ball, or you might find yourself faced with impossible odds. Jacob shares a story of grace under fire, acceptance with compassion and hope for a brighter future. Read his story in *From Diagnosis To Destiny* and refer to the insights often—you will never be the same, only better for it. Thank you, Jacob!"

— **Mark LeBlanc**, CSP
Author of *Never Be The Same*

"*From Diagnosis To Destiny* is a thoughtful, honest, real, and raw account of how Jacob 'JT' Thompson discovered what it means to trust the purpose of God for our lives, even when that purpose is discovered through difficulty and hardship. JT's love of the gospel, personal account of his road to salvation, passion for spoken word, and hopeful look toward the future spills forth onto every page. This is a must-read book for youth groups, parents, pastors, coaches, and every person looking for a reason to believe that God is in control, even when the road ahead is uncertain. A great book, written by an even greater man."

— **Laurel Bunker**
National Speaker, Educator and Pastor

FROM
DIAGNOSIS
TO DESTINY

YOUR TRIALS AREN'T MEANT
TO BREAK YOU;
THEY'RE MEANT
TO MAKE YOU!

JACOB "TEN20" THOMPSON

True Potential
REACH THE WORLD

From Diagnosis to Destiny
Your Trials Aren't Meant to Break You; They're Meant to Make You!

Cover and Interior Page Design by True Potential, Inc.

ISBN: 978-1-953247-49-0 (paperback)
ISBN: 978-1-953247-50-6 (ebook)

Library of Congress Control Number: 2021922749

True Potential, Inc.
PO Box 904, Travelers Rest, SC 29690
www.truepotentialmedia.com

Produced and Printed in the United States of America.

I dedicate this book to my father, Dr. James Dow Thompson. Dad, you are a great man and have been an amazing father. I look up to you in so many ways and have learned so much from you. You have shown me what it means to be responsible, to work hard, to have fun, and to put others before yourself. You have left a legacy for me that I hope to pass on to my own sons. I pray that through my life, you can see Jesus, and that you too will embrace His love for you and His plan for your life.

Boston Grey, Corey Graffeo, and Cooper Carroll, stay strong my young brothers. God has a purpose for you.

In loving memory of Coho Menk. Coho, thank you for helping me to open up and accept God's grace into my heart. I wish you could read this book, but I know that instead, you have been watching it from Heaven. That, my friend, is even better. That gives me peace.

ACKNOWLEDGMENTS

Mom and Dad, thank you for bringing me into this world and for raising me. Mom, thank you for bringing me to church and saying prayers with me at night. Dad, thank you for teaching me the value of hard work and getting the job done. Thank you for making me return the baseballs I stole from my team's bucket when I was 12 and then taking me to Dick's Sporting Goods to buy a bag of my own.

Abigail, thank you for bearing with me for the last 8 years. Thank you for sticking by me in good times and bad, for always encouraging me while keeping me humble at the same time, and for being my best friend.

John, Kristin, and Rick, thanks for being great siblings and putting up with me all these years. Thanks for enduring all the times I tried to get you to play with me as any good, annoying little brother would do. Thanks for always being there whenever I need anything.

Randy, Barb, and the rest of the Bircher family, thank you for raising an amazing daughter and welcoming me into your family.

Brett Theisen, Jordan Moberg, and Nels Leafblad, thanks for giving up your precious time to hang out with a bunch of goofy teenagers and tell us about Jesus.

Alex Hunter, thank you for pulling my gifts out of me and always helping me chase my dreams in whatever way possible.

Nathaniel Van Loon, thank you for being a great friend and my roommate of three years straight. You have always been there to encourage me in my faith, hold me accountable, and support me in my pursuits.

Andrew O'Reilly (AO), thanks for being a great friend, assistant coach, and ministry partner. I will always remember the day we tried to film my first spoken word video, but your phone died due to the below 0 temperature. Thanks for letting me hold onto you for stability, so I could see the view on top of Harney Peak.

Nathaniel and AO, thank you for reading through this book and giving me great feedback, and for allowing me to be part of the greatest article that Bethel University's *The Clarion* has ever seen.

Nathaniel, AO, Alex, Jake Toedter, Devin Nelson, and Phil Peterson, thank you for two years in the Clubhouse that I will forever cherish.

Wayne Andersen, thank you for being a great mentor, co-laborer, and friend.

Walt McFadden, thank you for being a faithful pastor and a spiritual guide to me, and for always leading by example.

Clover, Rachel, and the entire Carroll family, thank you for being such an encouragement to me personally, spiritually, and vocationally. Thank you for giving so much of your time and resources to help make the vision that God put in my heart a reality. Thank you for hosting me in your home and introducing me to Blue Bell Ice Cream. Hopefully, someday, I can introduce you to Tater Tot Hotdish.

Pastor Laurel Bunker and Dr. Claudia May, thank you for encouraging me in my gifts and giving me opportunities to use them.

Benny Roberts, thank you for producing and engineering my first EP, *No Excuses*, and for being a godly example of a husband, father, and minister.

Toey Lidstone, thank you for shooting my first spoken word poetry video, *The Cure*.

TJ Valtierra, thank you for bringing me to the studio with you after we had just met and inviting me into so many opportunities to share my music.

Coach Jim Galvin, thank you for being a great coach and for giving me my first opportunity to coach high school football.

Thank you, Jonathan Goff and Drew Grenand, for believing in me and inviting me into my first opportunities to lead ministry.

Hope Ledeboer-Smith, thank you for giving me my first real job and being such a steadfast and faithful leader.

Marquise Dixon, thank you for being a great mentor and older brother in the faith, and for taking me out on countless $1 taco and horchata dates and fulfilling my never-ending requests for letters of recommendation.

Marcos Canahui, thank you for hosting me in your home, showing me what is truly important in life, and being my first promoter as a *rapero*.

Spencer Sulflow, thank you for shooting and editing the *Keep on Fighting* video completely for free; it was an honor to be filmed by someone so talented.

Ben Hansen, thank you for approaching me and offering to edit this book, and helping me to get it published. Without you, this book would likely still be just an idea in my mind.

Steve Spillman, thank you for believing in me, encouraging me, and providing me with an opportunity to have this book published. May this be the beginning of a great partnership.

To those who haven't been named, you know who you are. Thank you to so many great family members, friends, mentors, coaches, teachers, professors, and brothers and sisters in Christ who have been integral parts of my journey.

None of this would have been possible without you.

CONTENTS

Preface...11

Prelude...12

Chapter 1   Forming My Identity...13

Chapter 2   A Shaky Foundation...22

Chapter 3   A Spark...27

Chapter 4   Backwards...35

Chapter 5   Reborn...42

Chapter 6   A New Beginning...50

Chapter 7   Freshman Lessons...55

Chapter 8   Training Grounds...65

Chapter 9   Una Adventura...75

Chapter 10   Real Men...83

Chapter 11   What Do You Want to Be When You Grow Up?.....90

Chapter 12   The Calm Before the Storm...101

Chapter 13   Time to Face the Music...107

Chapter 14   The Storm...111

Chapter 15   A Firm Foundation...119

Chapter 16   Hungry for Hope...126

Chapter 17   Michael Jordan...135

Chapter 18   Commit to Live...146

Closing Thoughts...162

Epilogue...166

PREFACE

From Diagnosis To Destiny. Wow. That is a weighty title. It makes it seem like I think I'm special or that I've done something extraordinary. I struggled with whether or not to write this book for that very reason. I don't think I'm special. I know for certain that I'm not perfect. And I haven't necessarily done anything extraordinary.

I haven't climbed Everest or pulled anyone out of a burning building. I didn't write this book so you could see me as a hero. I didn't write it as someone who went through a challenge and now is on the other side. I'm right here, stuck in the middle of my situation. I have days when I feel I can conquer the world and days when I just want to escape my reality.

But I do have something. Something that everyone needs, especially in a time such as this.

That something is hope.

My prayer is not that after reading this book, you think of me as some great person. My prayer is that you also would have hope.

Hope to endure whatever you are facing or will face.

Hope that brings you joy and peace.

Hope that helps you find your purpose, your destiny.

PRELUDE

In that one moment, it felt like my whole life up until that point finally made sense. All my questions were answered. All my wondering, resolved. All my confusion, explained. On the one hand, I was relieved to have a diagnosis. I now had a reason for why things were the way they were.

On the other hand, though, the diagnosis was devastating.

I'll be in a wheelchair?

I'll have trouble talking and even swallowing?

All my hopes and dreams were torn away from me with two simple words: *Friedreich's Ataxia.*

The career I pictured for myself…

The thought of playing with my kids and coaching their sports teams…

Over.

What is my purpose now? Is my life even worth living? One out of fifty-thousand—how can this be happening to me?

God, where are You?

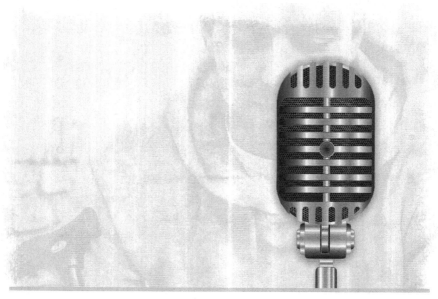

CHAPTER 1

FORMING MY IDENTITY

**Direct your children onto the right path, and when they are older, they
will not leave it.**
— Proverbs 22:6

See growin' up, church was now and then
I thought God was real, but never did allow Him in
I hated waking up Sundays and showerin'
Like, "gotta go to church, really mom, wow again?"
See Saturday nights I was home after curfew
But Sunday morning I'm sittin' in the church pew
I never paid attention, I'd probably fall asleep
The words of the sermon never really hit me deep
A young boy more focused on the temporary
Deeper thoughts about my purpose? That was secondary

Just tryna take the pretty girls on a date and
Hoping you could "watch a movie" in the basement

An excerpt from "the real me," a spoken word poem by TEN20

THE PEN

Throughout this book, you will get to know my love for metaphors and the profound life lessons that can be learned from insignificant objects and daily happenings—like learned lessons from a pen. As a kid, I loved taking things apart and putting them back together. In 5th grade I was kicked out of class for disassembling and reassembling my pen while the teacher was talking.

When you take a pen apart, it usually has about 4–7 pieces—basic pens that is, not go go gadgets. Now imagine if I disassemble the pen, put the pieces into a paper bag, and then shake the bag. What will happen? Will a pen come out of the bag? No. The result is always the same: no pen, just pieces.

> If something as simple as a pen cannot occur at random, I propose to you that *you* cannot either. You must have been designed intentionally; you must have a creator, and that creator must have a purpose in mind for you.

This experiment gives me the following insights into the pen. The pen is not an accident, nor did it come about at random. The pen must have been created and, therefore, have a creator. The pen has a purpose. The creator formed the pen intentionally with that purpose in mind. All pens have the purpose of writing, but all will write something different. Some will write stories while some will write poems. Some will grade papers, and others will jot down grocery lists. Whichever function they serve, the truth about them remains. They were created *on purpose* and *with purpose*.

How about you? Are you here at random? Do you have a purpose? The pen is 4–7 pieces; you are trillions. If something as simple as a pen cannot occur at random, I propose to you that *you* cannot either. You must have been designed intentionally; you must have a creator, and that creator must have a purpose in mind for you.

I am going to tell you my story—my journey with my creator and my purpose. My hope is that my journey may partner with yours, and together we can walk the paths of our destinies.

https://www.instagram.com/p/CHQRTB9hmU1/

For we are God's handiwork, created in Christ Jesus to do good works, which God prepared in advance for us to do (Ephesians 2:10).

WWII, A CAR CRASH, AND A GUMMY WORM

Life itself is a miracle. Our bodies need oxygen to function. They're sort of like bone-in chicken wings. We eat the chicken off the bones. The delicious chicken, fried in the Colonel's secret recipe, provides nourishment for our bodies. Then, we throw away the bones—or if we're environmentally conscious, we put them in our composts! Our bodies breathe in oxygen, use it to keep working, and then throw away the leftovers as CO_2. Sure enough, trees need CO_2 to survive! They eat up our CO_2 and then throw away more oxygen for us to breathe in! It is a beautiful, symbiotic relationship.

This is just one of countless examples of how our universe has been intricately designed for the sustenance of life. Think of the body's extremely complex systems, the miracle of birth, the perfectly calculated orbit of the earth around the sun, and so much more!

Not only is life a miracle, generally speaking, but also the fact that I am here and alive is a gigantic improbability. Before having any children, my grandfather was shot through the chest in World War II. One bullet went into his chest and out his back. Another passed through his thigh. One of his comrades threw him in a Jeep and drove him two hours across a European highway to the nearest hospital, where his life was saved by emergency surgery. My grandfather, Dr. John Rutherford Thompson, survived and went on to marry and have four children, one being my dad.

My dad, following in John R's footsteps, also became a doctor. One morning, he was driving home following an overnight shift and a mind-numbing morning meeting—who schedules those? He was exhausted. As he drove down an open road, going about 55 miles per hour, he drifted off to sleep. He "randomly" awoke as he was about 60 feet from the rear end of a stopped semi-truck. He slammed his brakes but went barreling into the semi. No one was hurt in the accident, except for his car. Had he not "randomly" awakened—I do believe God woke him—he most likely would have been beheaded by the semi's trailer.

My dad went on to marry my mom and, eventually, I came along on December 23, 1993. My mom made it back home in time to host Christmas Eve, which remains a family tradition today.

One fine afternoon, my dad, my brother John, and I were riding in our green Jeep Grand Cherokee and had to stop for gas. Per usual, I begged my dad to buy us a snack. This occasion was one of the 1% of the times that he actually agreed—thankfully so or I'd be overweight and unhealthy! My brother and I hopped back into the car, gummy worms in our hands and smiles on our faces. My brother resumed the "shotgun" position, and I sat in the back, behind the driver's seat. I watched John, who I secretly looked up to, as he slid whole gummy worms between his lips, slurping them into his mouth. For whatever reason, I assumed he wasn't even chewing them; I thought he was swallowing them whole. Note that we're talking full-sized gummy worms here—much bigger than their counterpart: the sour worm.

I was impressed and inspired. Wanting to be just like my older brother, I attempted the whole-gummy-worm-swallow for myself. One made it past. Then, another. I was feeling fairly confident at this point. And as I have often seen in my life, that's usually when things go completely wrong. The third oversized sugar-cylinder lodged in my esophagus. I couldn't breathe. I couldn't make a sound. I didn't know what to do. My dad drove along while John demolished his sugar intake for the week. After a while, my dad miraculously noticed my silence.

"Is Jake okay?"

John looked back to check on me. He didn't say a word. He looked at my dad and shook his head.

My dad yanked the Cherokee off the road, teleported right outside the backseat, opened my door, and slammed the heel of his hand between my shoulder blades as if he'd combined the force of all my life's spankings into one hit. The gummy worm escaped my airway and went airborne in slow motion across the Jeep's interior, just missing John's head. My life was spared.

From these three stories, I can see how very easily I could not be here today. And these are just the ones I know about. Imagine the countless near-death experiences throughout the generations. It is incomprehensible.

Life is a miracle. It is not to be taken for granted. Tomorrow is not to be assumed. Life is also fragile. I'll never forget the call I got from one of my best childhood friends, Coho Menk. Coho was a national champion speed skater and standout all-state soccer player. He was an amazing athlete but an even better person. He was calling me after his graduation from Baylor University, where he decided to study neuroscience after developing epilepsy in his late teens. He had plans to go on to graduate school and help people like himself. We made plans to hangout later in the week while he was home for break. The next day, I got another call from another high school friend. Coho had passed away. An epileptic seizure had seized the life from his body in his sleep.

> Life is a miracle. It is not to be taken for granted. Tomorrow is not to be assumed. Life is also fragile.

I learned that any day could be your last. Even today.

I believe it's a good investment of our time to try and figure out why we are here, before it's too late.

I pray that as we journey together through this book, we'll come one step closer to the answer.

The Son is the image of the invisible God, the firstborn over all creation. For in him all things were created: things in heaven and on earth, visible and invisible, whether thrones or powers or rulers or authorities; all things have been created through him and for him. He is before all things, and in him all things hold together (Colossians 1:15–17).

An Unpleasant Surprise

"Close your eyes and open your mouth." When the oldest and coolest kid in the neighborhood asks you to do something, you do it—especially when you're the youngest and least cool kid who just wants some approval. As I closed my eyes and opened my mouth, I felt something soft and mushy on my tongue. It tasted horrible.

Rabbit poop.

As I spit it out, I felt a mix of emotions—anger, sadness, betrayal. I left and went home crying… again. Being the youngest kid in the neighborhood who followed his older brother and his friends around, I endured this kind of bullying on a regular basis. Made fun of. Pushed around. Shot in the face at point blank with an airsoft gun. I was too small to fight back. Although my brother would stand up for me, he could do only so much, and I often left with my feelings hurt. Such were my early years in the neighborhood.

Gym Class Hero

Everything changed when I finally started kindergarten and got to be with other kids my age. On the first day of school, I met Riley on the bus, and we quickly became best friends. Early in the school year came the day for fitness testing. I jumped up on the pullup bar and did more pullups than my 5-year-old brain could count. When I got down, everyone was amazed. "You did 16, Jake!" the teacher exclaimed. "That's a school record!"

> I endured this kind of bullying on a regular basis. Made fun of. Pushed around. Shot in the face at point blank with an airsoft gun. I was too small to fight back.

At that time, the moment seemed insignificant—I now realize it was a turning point in my life. For the first time, I was experiencing acceptance and approval from my peers. It felt great, especially in contrast to the bullying I had endured. The acceptance, of course, was based on my ability to perform. So even at five years old, I was beginning to form my identity on what others thought of me.

As the years went on, I continued on this trajectory. My dad worked out with one of our neighbors—a former NFL player—who now coached the neighborhood sports teams. He must have seen potential in me because when I was in kindergarten, he let me play on the 2nd/3rd-grade baseball team that his son and my brother played on. After playing with older kids, playing with my peers became easy. I excelled in the sports I played and also won the presidential fitness award every year, resetting the school pullups record each year of elementary school. Sports were where I made friends and formed my identity.

Though gym class was going great, I had become quite the troublemaker in school. I was loud, disruptive, rebellious, and even got into a couple of fights. This didn't fly with my parents. I had a solid home life—my dad was an ER doctor and my mom was a lawyer and law professor. Both took education very seriously. My parents raised me well and taught me to be respectful. My mom brought me to church regularly and made sure I prayed before dinner and before bed. I knew it was wrong to act up in school, but I enjoyed the attention and popularity that my behavior brought.

I spent a lot of time with Riley, whose parents were far less strict than mine. At his house, we'd stay up late, watch R-rated movies, and go out ding-dong ditching. Though I got in trouble at school and was punished by my parents, I continued to misbehave. After all, it made my peers accept me, and my popularity only increased. For me, that was what mattered most.

These same patterns continued through middle school. I got in trouble regularly and didn't put forth much effort when it came to academics. But when it came to sports, it was a different story.

BIG DREAMS

I'll never forget when my coach pulled me aside when I was 11 years old after the Little League baseball season had ended. I had led my team in almost every offensive statistic. My team had just won the league championship, and I had been awarded the game ball. After the game, Coach tapped me on the shoulder and said, "Jake, you're the most consistent hitter I have ever seen. I truly believe you could play pro baseball someday." Maybe he was exaggerating or maybe he didn't know what he was talking about, but as an 11-year-old, I took every word of what he had just said to heart.

My athletic success continued through middle school. In 7th grade, I won 1st place in my school's annual pentathlon. One day during the summer heading into 8th grade, my brother had some friends over. They wanted to play touch football in the backyard but were one guy short, so they asked me to play. After scoring several touchdowns that day, I decided to sign up for the football team.

From the moment I put football pads on, I felt I had found who I was. The first time I crossed the goal line in a real game was unlike any feeling I had ever felt before. I ended up playing on offense, defense and special teams, never leaving the field, scoring a touchdown in every game. That year, Riley and I drifted apart, and I was making a new best friend, Ty.

Ty and I were inseparable. Football, baseball, Xbox, chasing girls, bike rides to the candy store—we did everything together. Our parents went to the same church, so Ty and I went through confirmation together. The period leading to confirmation was a time for all boys our age to come together and learn about our faith. But I was much more concerned about sports, girls, and friends than learning about God. So, confirmation became just another place for me to act out, get in trouble, make people laugh, and get attention from my peers.

In the summer heading into high school, I signed up for weight training, which all football players were expected to do. I worked out all summer. I loved that I was getting stronger and had something I was excelling in.

By the end of that summer, it was time for football relays, which was an annual weight lifting and running competition for football players. It was my school's version of the NFL combine. Participants were scored on a point system, and the top 10 in each grade were announced at back-to-football night in front of all the players and their parents. I went to a fairly big high school that played in the highest division in the state, so making the top 10 was a great accomplishment. At the end of football relays, I placed 3rd. Only one person barely beat me in the 40-yard dash: Ty.

NOT INTERESTED

During my freshman year, football, baseball and hockey were all coming along very well. Aside from sports, something unexpected was happening. Two guys, Theis and Moberg, as we knew them, coached the freshman football and baseball teams. There was something different about them; they were always in a good mood, didn't tear down their players, and seemed to take a genuine interest in our lives beyond sports. They would invite us out to eat, or to the park, or to play basketball.

Eventually, they invited us to something called Young Life. They didn't describe exactly what it was, but I knew it had something to do with God. After my time in conformation classes, I wasn't interested in going to anything that had to do with church. Also, I had my first high school girlfriend, and although we hadn't had sex, we were doing a lot of things I knew we shouldn't be doing. I didn't want to go to any church thing and be told to change my lifestyle, so I declined the invitation again and again.

My sophomore year, everything was going great. I had a starting position on the football team, a great group of friends, and a new girlfriend who went to a different school. Most of the popular girls at my school were innocent and weren't into hooking up with guys. At the Catholic school nearby, this wasn't the case. Before long, my girlfriend and I were doing just about everything but having sex.

> After my time in conformation classes, I wasn't interested in going to anything that had to do with church.

The summer heading into my junior year, Ty and I played on a summer baseball team, and I was having one of the best seasons of my life. We were also training for football, getting stronger every day, and I would surely place high in football relays again. We had a solid group of friends that played sports, chased girls, and caused shenanigans together. I had been with my girlfriend for almost a year. I had lost my virginity to her and thought we were in love and would be together forever. Sports were good. Friends were good. My girlfriend was good. I was good.

Then, one by one, things started to fall apart.

CHAPTER 2

A SHAKY FOUNDATION

"Therefore everyone who hears these words of mine and puts them into practice is like a wise man who built his house on the rock. The rain came down, the streams rose, and the winds blew and beat against that house; yet it did not fall, because it had its foundation on the rock. But everyone who hears these words of mine and does not put them into practice is like a foolish man who built his house on sand. The rain came down, the streams rose, and the winds blew and beat against that house, and it fell with a great crash."

— Luke 7:24–27

It's all fun and games until you involve your heart
Give it away just to watch it get broke apart
You were close, but with time, you grow apart
Fake smile on your face though, they can't know it's hard
So she's gone and I'm looking for the newer thing

Up late, looking at computer screens
No one can know, keep this history deleted
Know it's wrong, try to stop, but the action gets repeated
See I was empty, tryna fill the void
But my methods never worked, like they were unemployed
I acted like it was cool, like I wasn't annoyed
Try to ignore it but, it's something that you can't avoid
I kept everything bottled up inside of me
But I came to find out the world lied to me
Tryin' everything it said would fulfill me
But I was lost, just looking for the real me

An excerpt from "the real me," a spoken word poem by TEN20

CHOCOLATE CRINKLES

People who know me well know that I have a bit of a sweet tooth. Ever since I can remember, my family has held to a Christmas tradition of baking cookies and decorating the Christmas tree. Each kid in the family had *their* cookie. Rick rolled the coconut balls, John baked the sugar cookies, Kristin mixed the fudge bites. My cookie was the Chocolate Crinkle. To this day, Chocolate Crinkles are my favorite Christmas cookie. They are basically a soft, circular, powdered sugar covered brownie. They are delicious.

The recipe calls for unsweetened baking cocoa. One year, though, I was making the dough and this cocoa was nowhere to be found. No problem. I searched the pantry and found a bag of chocolate chips. This seemed like the perfect substitute. Not only were they chocolate, but they were much sweeter than the baking cocoa. I figured they would make the Chocolate Crinkles even better, if that were even possible. When I opened the oven, I immediately realized just how mistaken I was. These were no Chocolate Crinkles at all. They were completely flat and discolored. They tasted like stale crackers. And no, they were not sweeter either.

Recipes are not so easily modified, especially when it comes to baking. When cooking, it's easy to add some salt and pepper to taste. But change the foundational ingredients, and you will not be successful. The recipe exists for a reason.

God has given us a recipe for life in the Bible. One of the foundational ingredients is to find fulfillment and satisfaction in a relationship with Him, not in the pleasures of the world. Just like chocolate chips, some alternatives often seem more appealing than what God has put in His recipe. Therefore, it is easy to suppose that a sweeter ingredient will lead to a more enjoyable end result. In reality, it never does.

The promise of fulfillment and satisfaction made by sinful pleasures always comes up empty. Sex (outside of marriage), substance abuse, pornography, fame, money, success—none of these get the job done. God's recipe for our lives is not intended to deprive us of fun or make us miserable. On the contrary, He loves us and knows what is best for us. Have you ever tried plain baking cocoa? It doesn't taste very good. In the end, though, when the recipe is followed properly, the end result is fantastic.

Unfortunately, some lessons have to be learned the hard way.

> *Jesus answered, "Everyone who drinks this water will be thirsty again, but whoever drinks the water I give them will never thirst. Indeed, the water I give them will become in them a spring of water welling up to eternal life"* (John 4:13–14).

HEARTBREAK

I had built my foundation and identity on playing sports, girls liking me, and being popular. These were the things I cared about. The first brick to fall was the girl. My girlfriend and I had been together for more than a year. One day, she came over. We had the whole day to hang out. I planned on it being a regular day—a boat ride, a "movie," dinner, etc.

Right when she came over, I could tell something was off. She said we needed to talk.

"I think we need to take a break."

The words sunk in like a knife. Covering my hurt with anger, I lashed out. I told her I would be fine without her, she would miss me, and that she could leave. Once she was gone, the tears began to flow. It was like she had ripped my heart out, and I was left with a big hole inside. I thought maybe a new girl could fill that hole. With my friends, I acted like I was fine. "I'm back in the game," I told them. In reality, I had a void I was trying to fill. And as I bounced around in different relationships with different girls, I found out quickly that a new girl couldn't fill the hole in my heart. I had been introduced to pornography when I was 12, but now I was watching it more and more often. Though I knew it was wrong, and I knew the way I was treating girls was wrong, I was broken and trying to find healing. Nothing worked.

BROKEN DREAMS

Sports were the next thing to crumble. At the end of the baseball season, we had individual meetings with our coaches. The varsity head coach told me I had a great season and was an excellent offensive player. He said if I worked on my defense, I could probably play varsity in the upcoming season as a junior. After all the individual meetings, though, Coach gathered the team and announced that he wouldn't be returning and would be moving on to a college coaching job. With a new coach, I never got that shot at varsity, despite having a good tryout and hitting well on JV. Though I continued to play well on

One of the foundational ingredients is to find fulfillment and satisfaction in a relationship with Him, not in the pleasures of the world.

offense, my throwing started to get worse. I was having trouble finding my arm strength, and my accuracy was off. Something just didn't feel right, but I couldn't pinpoint what it was.

As a 17-year-old, senior year football feels like the pinnacle of your life. I had spent the last four years of my life preparing for the next three months. By attending a big high school, most players don't start on varsity until senior year. I had played well as a junior on JV and figured this year would be my year.

Ty and I worked out hard all throughout the off-season heading into our senior year. We even attended a tri-school lift/run/jump competition in which I had won first place in my weight class. When football relays came around, I felt confident I would hit the top 10 yet again. I took off on my 40-yard dash. "5.05," Coach said as I crossed the finish line. *What? 5.05? My freshman year, I ran a 4.99. Last winter, I ran a 4.80. That must have been a bad one. I'll try again.* I tried and tried but couldn't get any faster. *What's going on?* When it came time for my max lifts, I couldn't put up the numbers I had put up at the winter competition. I was weaker and slower, even after working out all year. I couldn't figure out what was happening.

I competed during training camp and saw the field a decent amount in our first couple of games. After that, though, I got beaten out of a starting position. I had to watch the game I loved and had poured my life into for the last four years from the sideline. Meanwhile, Ty was having a breakout season. The days when we tied for first in team races and dominated games together were over. Ty was faster, stronger, and was having great success on the field. Though I was happy for Ty, I was having an identity crisis. I didn't know why I couldn't perform like I knew I could, and I began to question who I was if I wasn't a star athlete.

> My dreams of going on to play in college and professionally were now just that—dreams. I sat in my room and wept as another piece of myself slipped through the cracks.

Our team went on to a 9-2 record, losing by 7 points in the section championship, and coming one TD short of setting the all-time school record for least points allowed. In the Spring, when baseball rolled around, both Ty and our other best friend, Pat, decided not to play. Pat got a job and Ty ran track, so I decided to play JV tennis for fun.

Then one day it all hit me, and I broke down. On the first day of freshman year, our gym teacher had asked us to write down how we wanted to be remembered when we left high school. I had written "number 23 on the football team." I had come from a line of Division 1 college athletes. My dad was a wrestling state champion and had received a scholarship to the University of Nebraska. His dad was the starting point guard on the Nebraska basketball team for three years. My great uncles were quarterbacks at Nebraska; one played in the Rose Bowl and another was a team captain.

Who was I?

I didn't even get to start in a varsity sport.

All my best friends were the stars of their respective teams, and I was playing JV tennis as a senior. My dreams of going on to play in college and professionally were now just that—dreams. I sat in my room and wept as another piece of myself slipped through the cracks.

What is my identity?

What is my purpose?

Do I even matter?

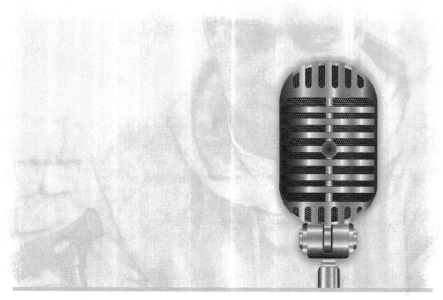

CHAPTER 3

A SPARK

For our God is a consuming fire.

— Hebrews 12:9

What's the meaning of life? Why are we here?
A question worth asking, but one many fear
But don't close your ear
Please hear
What I have to say and I will make it clear
Are we simply here to enjoy life on this earth till we die?
That just doesn't make sense, here is why
Why is there a hole in your heart that this world can't fill?
And you chase that thrill
Thinking this time it will

But it never does and you're left empty still

An excerpt from "Why?" a spoken word poem by TEN20

BASEMENT BALL

Have you ever been to a pro baseball game? Honestly, they can be pretty boring. Four hours watching a pitchers' duel, without food or drinks; after already buying tickets, my dad didn't want to pay for a $10 Maui Wowi smoothie too! One time, my dad and I were in the second row above the away team dugout. I had ceased to watch the seemingly best defensive—or worst offensive—baseball game ever played. When suddenly...

"Crack!"

Finally, a hit. I directed my attention back toward the diamond, but none of the players were reacting. In my peripheral vision, I noticed my dad ducking, hands over his head. I figured the ball must be headed in his direction. Naturally, I held my brother Rick's 13-inch glove over my dad's head. I hadn't brought my own glove, not wanting to risk forgetting it at the game. I had decided Rick's oversized glove would do.

> That day, Bert Blyleven—the "circle me Bert" guy—became my least favorite sports broadcaster of all time. "If you bring a glove that big to the game, you're supposed to catch the ball!" He chuckled, clearly entertained with himself.

I never even saw the ball. I just heard it ram into the empty seat two rows behind us. It was just a foul ball. The pitchers continued to duel. As my mind drifted back into my daydream, I was awakened from my mental slumber by my Motorola Razr flip-phone vibrating in my pocket. Text after text read, "are u at the Twins game?" Had this happened more recently, the texts would have included the laughing/crying emoji.

Rick had been watching the game from home and happened to be recording it on his fancy brand new DVR. The next time I was at his house, he played the recording for me. That day, Bert Blyleven—the "circle me Bert" guy—became my least favorite sports broadcaster of all time.

"If you bring a glove that big to the game, you're supposed to catch the ball!" He chuckled, clearly entertained with himself. It was my first (and last) time on national television. As if being an awkward middle-school kid with hockey hair, braces, and acne isn't bad enough. I had been roasted by circle me Bert.

All that said, pro baseball games weren't my favorite thing. But there can be an upside: souvenirs. If you're unlucky, you get a Lew Ford bobblehead that takes up space on your dresser until you move off to college and your mom throws it away while you're gone. If you're somewhat lucky, you get a Homer Hanky, which you can at least use to blow your nose in if the summer allergies get you. If you're extremely lucky, you get … drumroll, please … a wooden baseball mini-bat! Perfect for Basement Ball.

It all started with a mini-bat, a Koosh Ball, and a rainy day that sent my friends and me down to the basement to try to think of a way to have fun. We decided to have batting practice. The pitcher stood at one end of the pool table while the batter stationed himself on the opposite side, lengthwise. The yellow couch that had outlived my grandmother and had somehow made it to our downstairs playroom served as a backstop.

At first, it was just pitching and hitting. It evolved. Whoever was batting made contact and took off as if running toward first base. The base runner made his way around the pool table while the outfielder maneuvered around the foosball table to retrieve the Koosh Ball. Ball in hand, he crow-hopped and whipped it at the base runner. He was too late. The runner dove head first into the yellow couch, which had now become home plate, and evaded the ball. Thus, Basement Ball was born.

Rules were quickly formed so Basement Ball could be played in an "orderly" fashion. There was a ledge half way up the wall that stood on the opposite side of the basement from the batter. If the ball made it over the ledge (fence) and under the ceiling, it was a homerun, and the batter could proudly trot around the pool table. If the ball hit the ceiling, it was to be played as a fair ball. The runner would race around the billiards rectangle and attempt a dive into the couch before the pitcher or outfielder could give them a Koosh Ball-sized bruise—my brother Rick once threw the ball so hard that it shattered a glass window pane that protected a picture above the couch. Three strikes or a ball caught in the air meant the batter was out. A ball that hit the left wall before the start of the ledge (3rd base line) or the right wall before the glass door (1st baseline) was a foul. A batter got two outs, then his inning was over. Whoever scored the most runs by the time we got bored was the winner.

Why did we need to make so many rules? So we could get the most out of the game. All good games have rules! Imagine basketball with no traveling, fouls, or goaltending. It would be chaos. People would get hurt! Any great game needs rules. The rules allow players to play the game the way that it was intended to be played. Thus, to enjoy the game to the fullest extent. And who knows how the game is supposed to be played? Its designer.

Some people—my younger self included—want to stay away from God and church because they believe the Bible is full of too many rules. God doesn't want us to have any fun. No sex before marriage. No getting drunk. No pornography. God is just a regular old fun sucker. This couldn't be further from the truth!

"The thief comes only to steal and kill and destroy; I have come that they may have life, and have it to the full" (John 10:10).

Some of us see God's rules as restrictive. They are. But not in the way that most people think. These rules aren't meant to restrict us from fun. They are meant to restrict us from harming ourselves and others! Not having sex outside of marriage restricts us from creating deep spiritual and emotional ties that are bound to be ripped apart when not protected by the covenant of matrimony. Not getting drunk restricts us from hangovers, deadly car accidents, poor decision making, and alcoholism. No pornography restricts us from developing a dangerous addiction that tears apart marriages and feeds the ever-growing industry of sexual slavery.

How about these rules? No murder. No coveting. No adultery. Love your neighbor as yourself. Imagine if everyone lived by God's rules. This world would be a much better and enjoyable place.

The more we seek God, the more we can see who He really is. We will see that His rules are ultimately for our benefit. We will want to obey.

You should try it out!

How can a young person stay on the path of purity?
    By living according to your word.
I seek you with all my heart;
    do not let me stray from your commands.
I have hidden your word in my heart

that I might not sin against you.
Praise be to you, Lord;
    teach me your decrees.
With my lips I recount
    all the laws that come from your mouth.
I rejoice in following your statutes
    as one rejoices in great riches.
I meditate on your precepts
    and consider your ways.
I delight in your decrees;
    I will not neglect your word (Psalm 119:9–16).

MY OCTOPUS TEACHER

In September of 2020, Netflix released a somewhat strange, yet fascinating film called *My Octopus Teacher*. The film is a lyrical documentary that captures South African filmmaker and diver Craig Foster's unexpected relationship with an octopus. *My Octopus Teacher* received raving reviews, including a 100% rating on Rotten Tomatoes. My family and I decided to see what all the buzz was about.

At one point in the film, the octopus becomes aware of a nearby predator, a pyjama shark. Fearing for its life, the octopus quickly forms a disguise, changing its pigmentation and wrapping itself in seashells. The shark can smell the octopus and knows it's close. It senses the octopus, and even rubs up against it. All the while, Mr. Pyjama Shark fails to see what is right in front of its face.

> I was searching for identity. For satisfaction. For purpose. I could sense they were available. Deep down, I could feel there was more to my life than what I was seeing.

What are you searching for? I was searching for identity. For satisfaction. For purpose. I could sense they were available. Deep down, I could feel there was more to my life than what I was seeing. I just couldn't figure out what it was. I was the pyjama shark, hunting for fulfillment, knowing it was close by, but unable to see what was right in front of me.

C.S. Lewis, one of history's great Christian thinkers, puts it this way:

> The Christian says, Creatures are not born with desires unless satisfaction for those desires exists. A baby feels hunger: well, there is such a thing as food. A duckling wants to swim: well, there is such a thing as water. Men feel sexual desire: well, there is such a thing as sex. If I find in myself a desire which no experience in this world can satisfy, the most probable explanation is that I was made for another world.

I longed to answer the deep questions of life. *What is my identity? What is my purpose? Do I even matter?* These questions have answers, but the answers can't be found in worldly pursuits. We must look beyond this world to the true world we were created for.

> *The purposes of a person's heart are deep waters,*
> *but one who has insight draws them out* (Proverbs 20:5).

An Invitation

While my identity was crashing down around me, something else was going on in my life that didn't seem like a big deal—at least not at that time. It all started with an invitation.

As I said before, two weird guys, Theis and Moberg, coached my football and baseball teams. They were always inviting us to Young Life, and I was always saying no. However, the invitations didn't stop after the sports season ended. *What is up with these guys? Why do they want us to hang out with them so badly? They must not have any friends their age.* I didn't get it, but eventually that didn't matter. Some of my good friends had accepted the invitation and had nothing but good things to say about Young Life. I also found out that a lot of the older football guys that I looked up to attended regularly. More importantly, a lot of cute, upperclassmen girls also attended.

Considering these factors, I finally decided to check it out. To my surprise, I actually had fun. I ate candy, played games, and talked with my friends. No one made me pray or read the Bible. Plus, it felt like the adult leaders actually *cared* about me and wanted to get to know me. At the end of the night, one of the leaders stood up in front of everyone and talked about Jesus. To this day, I can't remember a single word of his message; I just remember being in a loving, caring, positive environment and feeling I could be myself.

For some reason, that night of Young Life inspired Ty and me to sign up for Camp Wapo, the church camp I had gone to as a kid. But since we were now in high school, we wouldn't just be campers; we would be junior leaders. We'd spend half our time doing activities together with our peers and the other half of our time helping out the real leaders with their campers. I can't remember signing up or what we were thinking when we signed up, but the reality was we signed up and paid our fees. At this point, we were going to camp whether we wanted to or not.

A MISSTEP

When the week of camp finally came around, Ty and I realized we had a baseball tournament that weekend. Everyone was leaving on Saturday, but our parents decided they would drive us up Sunday night after the tournament in which we were to play three games. In my first at-bat of the day, I hit a double in the gap and was in scoring position. The next guy up got a hit, and the third base coach waved me home.

On a good baseball team, the on-deck batter will tell the runner whether or not he should slide at home plate—this is done with a hand signal. As I was running home, my teammate was giving me the signal to slide. However, right before I got home, the shortstop decided not to throw home, so my teammate changed the signal. At the last second, I decided not to slide. I hadn't noticed, but for whatever reason, home plate was elevated about one inch off the ground. Since I had changed my mind at the last minute, I took an awkward step onto home plate.

> While my identity was crashing down around me, something else was going on in my life that didn't seem like a big deal—at least not at that time. It all started with an invitation.

A pain like I had never felt before surged through my ankle. I got up and limped off the field, but I knew I had messed something up pretty bad. That day, we had only nine guys to play, so sitting out wasn't an option, no matter how bad it hurt. I proceeded to play the total of three games, feeling worse and worse as the day went on. By the time I got home, every step sent excruciating pain through my ankle. There was no way I could go to camp. I had to call Ty and tell him I was staying home, and he should head up without me. My dad, who is an ER doctor, told me it would likely keep getting worse before it got better. I limped up to my bed that night and was disappointed that I was missing out on this opportunity to go to camp with my best friend.

PLEASANTLY SURPRISED

When I woke up the next morning, I couldn't believe it: My ankle was almost completely better! My parents were shocked, too. I was planning just to lie on the couch and let my ankle finish healing, but my parents had other plans. I'm not sure if they had planned something special while I was gone or what, but they wanted me out of the house. Though I thought the ship to go to camp had sailed, my mom called and asked if I could still come up. Sure enough, they said yes, and next thing I knew, I was in the car on my way there.

To be honest, I wasn't looking forward to it. I didn't want to do too many activities and re-injure my ankle. Ty was the only person I knew there, and he was probably already making new friends. But, excited or not, we pulled up to the camp, I got out, waved goodbye to my mom, and off she went.

Just as I was pleasantly surprised when I had gone to Young Life for the first time, I never would have anticipated how much I enjoyed my week at camp. We did all kinds of fun activities together with other teens. Then, we spent time helping out the camp counselors with the kids in their cabins. I couldn't believe what one of the leaders was saying as I got to know him better.

He was wearing a football shirt, so he seemed like a cool guy to me. Turns out he had even won a state championship. I'm not sure how it came up in conversation, but he told me he had never kissed a girl! *What's wrong with this guy? Maybe he doesn't like girls?* He said he was "saving himself for marriage." This was basically the opposite of me and all of my friends, who desperately wanted to hook up with any cute girl who was willing.

As the week went on, I got to know more and more people like this leader— people who actually lived out what they said they believed. Something was going on in my heart that I couldn't describe. On the final night, the junior leaders and camp counselors stayed up late singing songs around the fire.

For the first time since I could remember, I felt free.
I felt free of what other people thought.
Free from past mistakes.
Free from keeping up a certain image.
Free from measuring myself by my performance.

As I stared into the fire, I felt an overwhelming sense of God's presence; it was unexplainable. I knew in my heart, for the first time, that God was real, and I was meant to follow Him for the rest of my life.

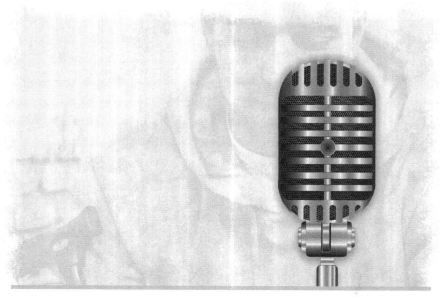

CHAPTER 4

BACKWARDS

"Woe to you, teachers of the law and Pharisees, you hypocrites! You clean the outside of the cup and dish, but inside they are full of greed and self-indulgence. Blind Pharisee! First clean the inside of the cup and dish, and then the outside also will be clean."

— Matthew 23:35–26

To make matters worse, what I thought was love had failed
She said "goodbye" and my life was derailed
Luckily I remembered what happened that summer when I felt God's Holy Spirit
I knew my only hope was to seek and grow near it
My mentors, friends and I started to study the Bible
It seemed as though that was my only chance for survival
I learned what it meant to be a man of God, how to follow the rules

But this led me to notice all of the other fools
I saw how they drank, smoked, and partied and I threw stones of condemnation
I thought I was a Christian because I didn't give in to the same temptation
I pretended I was this good person that would do no wrong
But I happily would have looked at a girl in a thong
I cleaned the outside of my cup and would have said in God I trust
But I went home every night and struggled with lust
I wore around a smile but it was really a mask
While I carried secret burdens of mistakes in the past

An excerpt from "Saved," a spoken word poem by TEN20

THROWING UNDER PRESSURE

When my dad was just a boy, his dad bought a piece of land in East Battle Lake in western Minnesota and built a cabin on it. The family would drive nine hours just to enjoy time at the lake—fishing, playing cards, and getting away from the regular hustle and bustle of life. The tradition has carried on. While I was growing up, my family would spend at least three weeks at the cabin every summer.

"Yeah, mom, you gotta learn to throw under pressure." The words left my mouth simultaneously as the ball left my hand.

One year, my friend Pat came along too. Pat and I had been friends since we were about 5 years old. We both played baseball and hockey and spent countless hours at each other's houses playing with—or more realistically, competing against—each other. A few cabins down, our neighbors had an old tennis court they let us use whenever we wanted. My whole family and Pat ventured up to the tennis court for some not-so-leisurely games. Pat and I brought our baseball gloves and a ball, so we could play catch when it was our turn to sit out.

On the south side of the court, there was a garage. In addition to what garages are normally used for, our neighbor used this garage as a woodshop. Between the court and the woodshop was a good-sized, double paned glass window. I was around 12 years old; an age when it's easy to forget that moms are almost always right. After a few back-and-forth throws, parallel to the court, my mom chimed in.

"Maybe you should move, so the window isn't behind Pat." I figured it was a decent idea.

"Yeah, bro, let's move to the other side."

"Come on, man," Pat responded. "You have to learn to throw under pressure." He was right.

"Yeah, mom, you gotta learn to throw under pressure." The words left my mouth simultaneously as the ball left my hand. I knew right away I was in trouble. Pat leaped in the air, but the ball was headed about a half inch over his outstretched glove. When I went to assess the damage, I learned for the first time what a double-paned window was. Two layers of glass had smashed all over the woodshop. After apologizing to the neighbor, cleaning the woodshop, a trip to the window store, and 14 hours of physical labor for my dad to pay him back for the new window, I had learned my lesson.

When you put all your focus on *not* doing the wrong thing, you usually end up doing it anyway. All my energy was focused on not hitting the window with the baseball. And where did I end up throwing it? Exactly.

If I had focused instead on throwing the ball directly to Pat's glove, I probably would have avoided the entire hassle that followed the window breaking. Unfortunately, this approach is often taken when it comes to faith. Faith is seen as a long list of rules. Don't do this. Don't do that. Don't have any fun. The items on the list of don'ts become the greatest temptations that we end up giving into. Instead, if we focused on the *do's* of faith, we would be much better off. Actively loving others, serving the needy, fellowshipping with our brothers and sisters, studying God's Word. If our focus were here, the rulebook would not be so tempting; it would likely be avoided altogether.

To do what is right and just is more acceptable to the Lord than sacrifice (Proverbs 21:3).

THE FIRST STONE

In Jesus' time, there was a group of men called Pharisees. These were the spiritual giants in Israel, where Jesus lived. To become a Pharisee, you had to memorize lots of Scripture and follow all kinds of strict rules. Because of this, people thought of the Pharisees as being close to God. When Jesus came, though, He exposed the truth about them. Jesus scolded the Pharisees for trying to look good on the outside but not having God's love in their hearts. They knew the right things to say and how to act in public, but they weren't changed on the inside.

Jesus had many harsh words for the Pharisees. He called them white-washed tombs. Ouch. They looked good on the outside, but on the inside, they were dead. Rotting bones. They were seeking approval from people rather than from God. Because of this, they hated Jesus. As Jesus went about healing the hurting, feeding multitudes, and giving awesome speeches, more and more people started following Him. He was going viral. Meanwhile, people were bringing up @ThePharisees on Instagram and hitting the unfollow button.

This made the Pharisees angry. They wanted Jesus to go away. He was way cooler than they were and, therefore, way more popular. They had to get rid of Him. So, they devised a plan.

"Let any one of you who is without sin be the first to throw a stone at her" (John 8:7).

One day, Jesus was hanging out in the Temple courts. People gathered around Him, as usual, and He taught them. This was home base for the Pharisees. This probably made them even more mad! This would be similar to your arch nemesis from a rival high school coming to your prom for a date with the girl you liked!

This was the perfect opportunity to trap Him. The Pharisees brought a woman whom they claimed to have just caught in the act of adultery—I have my doubts—and threw her on the ground before Jesus. They explained how the law of Moses commanded that this woman be executed by stoning. They asked Jesus what they should do.

They were asking with the intention of trapping Jesus by His own words. If he said that she shouldn't be executed, He would be guilty of breaking the law of Moses. If He said to execute her, He would lose the hearts of the people. A win-win for the Pharisees and a lose-lose for Jesus.

Or so they thought.

Their question was misguided, just like their hearts. They were asking Jesus to trap Him. They weren't asking because they wanted to know the truth. They weren't wondering what God thought about the situation. They had already made up their minds.

I have seen too many people ask questions of Jesus with this same misguided heart. *If God is so great, why_____. If God is real, how come _____.* Fill in the blank with whichever objection people like to raise against Jesus, the Bible, or God. When you start to respond with a reasonable answer, they have already stopped listening. They don't want the truth. They just want to justify their unbelief.

Check your heart.

> *Anyone who chooses to do the will of God will find out whether my teaching comes from God or whether I speak on my own* (John 7:17).

Back to the drama. Jesus, all eyes on Him, bent over and began chalking the sidewalk (actually he wrote in the sand, since chalk wasn't invented yet). I wonder what He was writing. Maybe He was biding His time, waiting for the Holy Spirit to give Him the right answer. Maybe He was writing down the woman's true identity, which she seems to have lost somewhere along the difficult road of life. Maybe he was just doodling. The Bible doesn't say.

When He arose, He gave the greatest mic-drop answer of all-time: *"Let any one of you who is without sin be the first to throw a stone at her"* (John 8:7). I can hear Welven Da Great in the background to all the Pharisees saying "got eemmm."

The Pharisees dropped their stones and walked away.

> *Jesus straightened up and asked her, "Woman, where are they? Has no one condemned you?"*
>
> *"No one, sir," she said.*
>
> *"Then neither do I condemn you," declared Jesus. "Go now and leave your life of sin"* (John 8:10–11).

Pay attention to the order of Jesus' words. First, He says that he doesn't condemn her. This woman would have been in a state of sheer terror. She was about to be brutally executed. Jesus had saved her life. He had chosen not to hold her sins against her. Imagine the relief she must have felt. You can bet that whatever Jesus was about to say next, this woman would take it to heart.

And what did He say?

Go and leave your life of sin.

In that order.

And that is what true Christianity is. It is not a heartless following of restricting rules. It is the acknowledgment that we have broken the rules and are deserving of God's wrath. But just before the first stone can be thrown, Jesus steps in and saves us. In our gratitude, we wait for His instructions. They are simple. Go and leave your life of sin.

At this point in life, though, I still didn't quite get it.

HYPOCRISY

I thought that following God meant trying to be a good person. I knew there were certain "sins" I shouldn't be doing, such as having sex, drinking, doing drugs, killing people, and things like that. I thought that as long as I avoided these "big sins," then I was good and God would accept me. I became what people thought of as a "good Christian kid." I stopped cussing, didn't go to parties, didn't do drugs, got straight A's, and was respectful to my teachers and coaches. I also started attending Young Life every week. It turned out that the week Ty and I were at Camp Wapo, some of our other friends had gone to Young Life camp with Theis and Moberg. After camp they started a Bible study that met every Sunday night. Throughout my junior and senior year of high school, I never missed Young Life or Bible study.

> Everyone thought of me as a good kid, but I knew deep down that in many ways, I was fake.

As I avoided the "big" sins of partying, drugs, and sex, I began to become very judgmental of those who partook in these things. As certain friends went further in this direction, I began to cut them out of my life. I became self-righteous and prideful, thinking I was better than people like that.

The problem was, I was still just as sinful. The only difference was, my sin was in private. I struggled daily with lust and pornography. I tried to resist, knowing it was wrong, but would always end up giving into temptation. I tried to fight my sin by my own strength but was never strong enough to conquer it. Additionally, I had never told ANYBODY that I had lost my virginity. I eventually became weighed down by the guilt of my sin. Everyone thought of me as a good kid, but I knew deep down that in many ways, I was fake. I had it all backwards.

So I find this law at work: Although I want to do good, evil is right there with me. For in my inner being I delight in God's law; but I see another law at work in me, waging war against the law of my mind and making me a prisoner of the law of sin at work within me. What a wretched man I am! Who will rescue me from this body that is subject to death (Romans 7:21–24)?

CHAPTER 5

REBORN

Therefore, if anyone is in Christ, the new creation has come: The old has gone, the new is here!
— 2 Corinthians 5:17

'Til one day, I couldn't take it anymore
See God had been knockin', I opened up the door
I confessed all my shame and my secrets
He told me He could take it, I didn't have to keep it
He said, "son, you're forgiven
That's why I've died and I've risen
So you could be free from that prison that you live in
All this time you've been looking for love
But I've always been there, and I'm more than enough"

An excerpt from "the real me," a spoken word poem by TEN20

THE SPATULA

Later in this book, I will describe the Thompson men camping trips and their epicness in greater detail. For now, though, I'll tell you a story. One year we were camping on the North Shore of Lake Superior in early June. Minnesota summers are beautiful, but that far up north, it never feels very warm. Not to mention, the water was freezing. No one dared take a leisurely float and catch some rays.

The only body part that intentionally entered the just-above-freezing water was the hand of whoever's turn it was to do dishes. It was custom for the lucky winner of any given meal to do the dishes right after the meal was over since we would soon need the dishes again for our next meal. Most prized of all dishes was none other than the spatula. The spatula flipped add-water pancakes, fresh fried fish, and summer sausage slices in a pan over a fire. It was *essential*.

They saw the spatula in my hand and knew exactly what I was thinking. "Don't do it," my dad urged.

One evening after dinner, we packed up the dishes for my dad and my brother John to take down to the lake and wash. At this campsite, we were up on a small cliff. There was a path around the side of the cliff down to the water. Those of us who weren't on dish duty were preparing the campsite for the evening when suddenly, I spotted what could have been a major problem: The spatula. The dishwashers had forgotten it. It sat there on a log, dirty from dinner preparations. Surely we would need the spatula the next morning to flip our pancakes. Who would want to flip pancakes with a dirty spatula that had sat out in the wilderness all night—that is, if it wasn't dragged away by a hungry animal? I had to do something. I snapped into action.

I grabbed the spatula and rushed toward the cliff, catching the attention of my dad and brother, who were almost done washing the dishes below. They saw the spatula in my hand and knew exactly what I was thinking.

"Don't do it," my dad urged. He knew I was planning to throw the spatula down to them. From my previous baseball-and-window story, you can imagine the reputation I gained as a bit of an "overthrower." My dad had even compared me to Chuck Knoblauch, the infamous Minnesota Twins player who developed the yips—basically, forgetting how to throw. I was in no mood for sound wisdom. The spatula needed to be washed, and there was no time to waste. I wound up and let the spatula loose.

As soon as the spatula left my hand, I turned and sprinted back to my tent. I didn't even need to watch. I knew I had made a grave mistake. The spatula was well on its way to being lost at sea. Arriving at my tent and rummaging through my backpack, I found a pair of shorts and threw them on. I ran down the path around the cliff to the water below. I dove straight in, and a few moments later, I had recovered the spatula and saved the day—from the problem I had created in the first place. To this day, my family laughs about this story. When my dad retells it, he never leaves out how I really "Knob-lauched" it.

For some reason, this story has always stuck with me. I think I know why now. I made a mistake. I should have listened to my dad. I should have walked down the path around the cliff and handed the precious spatula to the dishwashers. Instead, I thought I knew best.

> If we are honest with ourselves, we have all missed the mark with God. We have all "Knoblauched" it in our own ways. Our Father has told us how we ought to do things, but we think we know best.

The worst thing I could have done to compound my mistake was not to be willing to admit I had made one. I could have blamed whoever left the spatula behind, my dad, or my brother for not being able to jump higher—honestly, though, even LeBron James wouldn't have been able to catch that spatula. I also could have let the spatula drift off toward the middle of Lake Superior, and the rest of our trip could have been miserable and spatula-less.

Instead, I simply admitted my mistake and made a correction.

If we are honest with ourselves, we have all missed the mark with God. We have all "Knoblauched" it in our own ways. Our Father has told us how we ought to do things, but we think we know best. In our pride, we throw our proverbial spatulas into deep water. The spatula represents our purpose and our identity. Thinking we know best, we throw them away into deep waters instead of walking the more difficult path and handing them to our Father. If we don't make a correction, they will never be found again. Life will go on without the spatula. Without purpose. Without identity. Without hope.

The story of the spatula reminds me of the story Jesus told in the Gospel of Luke chapter 15. There is a father and two sons. The sons were set to split their father's inheritance when he died. The father owned land and had servants, so the inheritance was likely a lot of money! The younger son couldn't wait. Maybe you can relate. We want to enjoy life and we want to do it now. He asked his father to grant him his inheritance early. In other words, he said, "Dad, you're still alive, but you're dead to me. I don't want you anymore; I just want your money."

The father obliged.

Wow.

The younger son took off and spent all the money on his pleasures. Eventually, the money that was supposed to set him up for the rest of his life was gone. Then, famine hit the land and the only job he could get was feeding slop to pigs. He was so hungry that he even considered eating the pig slop!

When he came to his senses, he realized he had made a mistake. He realized how great his life was with his father. Even his father's servants were living better than he was. This younger son resolved to head home and beg for forgiveness. He prepared a speech to apologize to his father, but before he could utter it, the father ran to him, kissed him, gave him a brand new tuxedo, and threw a massive party. He was simply thrilled to have his son back.

The key turning point in the story is when the son comes to his senses. He admitted his mistake, and he sought correction.

The father was waiting with open arms.
The Father waits for you with open arms.
Just admit your mistakes. Just acknowledge that you "Knoblauched" it.
The Father is waiting for you. He is ready to wrap His arms around you and throw a party for you.
It's time to come home.

Unfortunately, this story doesn't end happily ever after for everyone. While the younger son had been out in the distant country blowing his inheritance, the older son stayed home and did what he was supposed to. He kept the rules. He worked hard. Hey obeyed.

When the older son found out that his brother came home and his father had thrown him a party, he was furious. And rightly so. If his father welcomed his younger brother back as a son, the older brother would now have to share his part of the inheritance with his brother. Some people know that family-and-money disputes tend to cause fierce disagreements, even broken relationships.

The older son refused to come to the party and celebrate.

The father came out to the elder son and beckoned him to join the celebration. "Your brother was lost, and now he is found. He was dead, and now he is alive." The son retorted he had been obeying the father for years and never got a party thrown for him.

Despite his father's beckoning, he still refused the invitation.

His actions revealed his heart. From the outside, the older and younger brothers looked like opposites. Beneath the surface, though, they were equivalent. The older son didn't love the father; he too just wanted the father's inheritance. He was more concerned about losing money than his brother's restoration.

Maybe you relate to the older son. You keep the rules and walk a relatively straight path. You do what you're supposed to do in hopes you will reap the rewards. You are a good person. But deep down, you don't love the Father.

You can't admit you have made a mistake.
That you have disobeyed the Father and tried to go your own way.
It all looks good on the surface, but your heart is not connected to the Father.
Don't stay outside the party.
Don't let your spatula sink into the depths.
Come home.

> *Say to them, 'As surely as I live, declares the Sovereign Lord, I take no pleasure in the death of the wicked, but rather that they turn from their ways and live. Turn! Turn from your evil ways! Why will you die, people of Israel* (Ezekiel 33:11)?'

GERMINATION

It is common knowledge that plants grow from seeds. In order for a seed to become a plant, it must go through the process of germination. When the seed goes into the ground, it is dormant; it has the potential for life within it, but it isn't actively living. The seed has a coat to protect itself. While in the ground, the plant embryo within the seed begins to grow. Eventually, the growing plant bursts out from the seed coat, searching for sunlight. At this point, the plant can grow and bear fruit, fulfilling its purpose.

We spend much of our lives building our own seed coats to protect ourselves. We don't want to be hurt by the actions or words of others. We want to feel safe. Like the seed, though, we are dormant; we have the potential for life within us, but we are not truly living. We are concerned about what other people think of us. We want to create a certain image. All the while, the potential for greatness is within us, wanting to escape.

> We want to feel safe. Like the seed, though, we are dormant; we have the potential for life within us, but we are not truly living.

To experience the life we are created for, we need to shed our seed coat of false identity and step into the light of the sun (Son). I had spent years building my seed coat, keeping my issues and my secrets trapped safely inside. It was time to shed my coat. It was time to step into the light. It was time to live.

Very truly I tell you, unless a kernel of wheat falls to the ground and dies, it remains only a single seed. But if it dies, it produces many seeds. Anyone who loves their life will lose it, while anyone who hates their life in this world will keep it for eternal life (John 12:24–25).

AN ADVENTURE

The summer after my senior year, my Bible study group, led by Theis and Nels, now one of our Young Life leaders for the past two years, took a trip to the Rocky Mountains in Colorado. The plan was to go whitewater rafting for one day, spend the night at base camp, and then hike through the mountains for five days. To my surprise, a couple of guys whom I never would have expected to sign up were coming on the trip with us. Two of the guys were Brian and Coho. Brian, Ty, and I had been best friends through middle school and early on in high school. Brian stopped playing football and baseball after freshman year. Naturally, we didn't see as much of him. Beyond this, he started hanging out with some of the guys on the lacrosse team, getting into drugs and partying. Our friendship had slowly drifted apart.

Coho had been one of my best friends throughout high school. We had played on hockey teams and church basketball teams together. We had countless sleepovers and great memories playing NHL (Chell) on Xbox and staying up way too late. However, toward the end of high school, he too had gotten into activities I wasn't interested in, and we had drifted apart as well. Though I was surprised, I was glad they were coming on the trip.

Whitewater rafting was amazing; we had so much fun. We spent the first night at base camp. The next day we were off on our hike through the mountains. This was the most hard-core camping I had ever done. We were doing "leave no trace" camping, so we didn't bring soap, deodorant, or even toilet paper.

> As we hiked across the Rocky Mountains, I wasn't feeling quite right. I was tired and dizzy. I was unbalanced and just felt "off."

As we hiked across the Rocky Mountains, I wasn't feeling quite right. I was tired and dizzy. I was unbalanced and just felt "off."

Though the hikes were difficult for me, we were all having a great time. The mountains were beautiful, the food was great, the weather was nice, and we were all catching up and having good conversations. Once we stopped and set up camp, Theis and Nels would give us a short list of Bible verses to read. We would each go off on our own to read the verses and have some time in prayer and solitude. At night, we would process what we read in the Word, and then one or two guys would share their life story with the group.

VULNERABILITY

I was one of the first guys to share my story, but I didn't really get deep. I talked about how I had encountered God at camp and how I had become a "better person." As the trip went on, guys' stories got deeper and deeper. One guy shared how he was drowning in an ocean current and a hand pulled him out; when he surfaced the water, no one was around. Another guy shared how he had been struggling with depression and thought about taking his life. I was amazed at how these guys were being vulnerable and opening up about things, and I started thinking about all the things that weighed on my heart that I was too embarrassed to share. Then it came time for Brian and Coho to share. I'll never forget what happened next.

WEIGHT LIFTED

Brian broke down into tears and shared all about how he had been partying, having sex, and smoking weed daily. Despite all of that, he said he was still unfulfilled and felt he was losing himself. Then Coho did the same thing. Through his tears, he opened up about all the things he had been struggling with and all the wrong things he had been doing.

In that moment, I realized this whole time I had been judging them instead of being the loving friend they needed. I started to feel a tug on my heart. These two guys were able to open up about their mistakes.

Maybe I could too.

No one knew I wasn't a virgin or that I had been struggling with pornography.

I decided to open up.

Tears began to stream down my cheeks as I confessed everything. Losing my virginity, struggling with pornography, feeling broken inside, and questioning my identity. All of a sudden, a literal weight was lifted from my shoulders, and an unknown sensation shot through my entire body. For the first time, I felt God's love and forgiveness wash through me from my head to my toes, making me clean. At that point, I knew something inside me had changed.

CHAPTER 6

A NEW BEGINNING

Don't let anyone think less of you because you are young. Be an example to all believers in what you say, in the way you live, in your love, your faith, and your purity.
— 1 Timothy 4:12

So I stopped waiting, I made the decision
He gave me a new life, new goals, new vision
Don't get me wrong, I'm far from perfect
But improving every day and I'm living with a purpose
Inside of me there's no more hole
I've got peace, love, and joy in my soul
He never leaves me, He stays close by
I found the real me, a son of the Most High

An excerpt from "the real me," a spoken word poem by TEN20

https://www.youtube.com/watch?v=A2GPHHB4sVI

BOUGHT WITH A PRICE

I am grateful for the many lessons my parents taught me while growing up, whether explicitly or implicitly. Of these many lessons, they taught me the value of money. My parents didn't buy me whatever I asked for. Instead, they gave me opportunities to earn money and then to spend it as I wished. I could earn an allowance by doing chores around the house—cleaning the bathroom, mowing the lawn, shoveling the driveway, etc. Then, I could spend my money freely.

> How much one values something is measured by how much one is willing to pay for it. The Bible is a love story about God paying for our redemption from sin with His only Son, Jesus, whose value is eternal.

As a young boy, I bought candy, pocket knives, and cap guns. As I got a bit older, I bought sports equipment, movie tickets, and yes, I still bought candy. One year in middle school, I spent every dollar I had on a Bauer Vapor XX hockey stick. The advertisements had sold me. I truly believed this stick would make me a better player. When you truly want something, you'll pay for it, even a high price.

The Bible explains that Jesus is eternal—He has no beginning and no end. John 3:16, perhaps the most famous verse in the whole Bible, says this: *"for God so loved the world that He sent His only son, that whoever believes in Him will not perish, but have eternal life."*

How much one values something is measured by how much one is willing to pay for it. The Bible is a love story about God paying for our redemption from sin with His only Son, Jesus, whose value is eternal. This act shows just how much God loves and values each one of us.

Following Jesus is not about trying to keep rules and earn favor with God. Rather, it's living out of the recognition that God loves us beyond measure and, therefore, seeking to please Him—to have a mutual loving relationship.

I now knew that God loved me, valued me, and forgave me. I had a new identity. A new purpose. I wanted to live for God. I wanted to share His love. And now, I would have an opportunity to do so.

> *For you know that it was not with perishable things such as silver or gold that you were redeemed from the empty way of life handed down to you from your ancestors, but with the precious blood of Christ, a lamb without blemish or defect* (1 Peter 1:18–19).

A TEXT THAT CHANGED MY LIFE

Just a few days after I got back from the backpacking trip, I got a text that changed my whole life. It was from one of my Young Life leaders: "Hey, would you like to come to camp next week and help lead a cabin of middle school boys?" I had chosen to attend Bethel University, the Christian college near where I had grown up, mainly because my Young Life leaders had gone there. I looked up to them so much, and now I was being invited to an opportunity to play that same role in someone else's life.

I didn't know the Bible very well or how to articulate any of my theological beliefs. But I knew I had encountered the love of the Father, and I was excited to share it with anyone and everyone.

I agreed to come to camp as a leader. I didn't know the Bible very well or how to articulate any of my theological beliefs. But I knew I had encountered the love of the Father, and I was excited to share it with anyone and everyone. This was the perfect opportunity.

After that camp opportunity, the Young Life head leader at Highview Middle School asked me to join his team to help lead throughout the year. I had such a great time at camp that I agreed. I was now in my first semester at Bethel University and was loving it. I attended chapel every Monday, Wednesday, and Friday, and vigorously took notes on everything I was learning. I resolved to read the entire New Testament and committed to praying and reading one chapter every day.

I had also committed not to have a girlfriend for at least one semester; I just wanted to focus on growing my faith. I started making great friends who also wanted to grow in their faith journeys. I recruited some of them to lead Young Life with me. On some Young Life program nights, I was the one giving the message about Jesus. This forced me even more to read my Bible to truly know what I was talking about. Toward semester's end, Jonathan, the head leader, told me he was graduating at the end of the year and moving away. He asked if I would take over for him. I agreed. Before I knew it, I was leading my very own ministry team.

RUSTY

One of the friends I recruited to lead Young Life with me was Devin Nelson. I met Devin on one of the first days of freshman year. I was in the dining center proudly wearing my Mounds View High School Football shirt when I saw another freshman guy wearing a Stillwater High School shirt—Stillwater was our high school's rival. Devin and I became friends instantly. We both loved to play sports, but neither of us played on a university team. We spent a lot of time working out and shooting hoops together.

When the time came, we decided to sign up for intramural flag football and draft a team. Luckily, I had my minivan and Bethel allowed me to keep it on campus for my ministry—freshmen aren't typically allowed to have a car on campus. Each week we'd pile our team into the minivan and go play our flag football game at a nearby park. Our team, The Slayers, ended up winning the championship all four years at Bethel. Devin and I were both average players but happened to recruit an all-star team.

During the first game of freshman year, I went to run my route, and when I tried to make a cut, I tripped and caught myself on the ground. *That was weird. Maybe it's because I haven't worn cleats in a while. Or maybe I'm just rusty.* I continued to play in the game without tripping again, but I still didn't feel quite right. I felt I had lost a step or two over the last year.

A GREAT START

The day that Devin and I became friends, he invited me that night to play sand volleyball. I had never played much volleyball but figured it was a good way to make friends. And I also figured there would likely be some pretty girls there. I was right about both. Soon there was a regular group of us who played almost every night. A few of those from that group are some of my best friends to this day, and one of them is my wife.

Abbie Bircher, now Abigail Thompson, was cute, smart, funny, nice, athletic, and had a true heart for God—everything I was looking for in my future wife. Luckily, she too had encountered the Lord shortly before coming to Bethel, and as fate would have it, she too had committed to the Lord not to date anyone during the first semester. We continued growing our friendship during that first semester, though, on some instances, it became obvious we were more than friends. On December 14, 2012, the last day of the first semester, we became official boyfriend and girlfriend. College was off to a great start. I had a girlfriend, a great group of friends, was leading a ministry, and was growing in my faith daily.

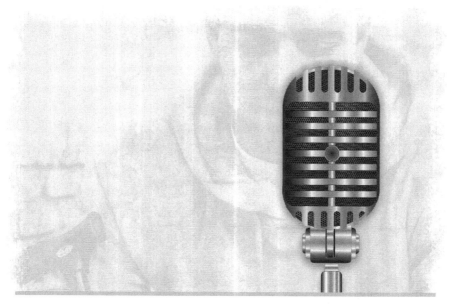

CHAPTER 7

FRESHMAN LESSONS

Therefore, I urge you, brothers and sisters, in view of God's mercy, to offer your bodies as a living sacrifice, holy and pleasing to God—this is your true and proper worship. Do not conform to the pattern of this world, but be transformed by the renewing of your mind. Then you will be able to test and approve what God's will is—his good, pleasing and perfect will.

— Romans 12:1–2

I will worship my lord with everything

But as I sing

On my heart is a heavy thing

Because there is a dying world right outside our doors

The people are lost, both the rich and the poor

And each one of them is deeply loved by my lord

So let us not shy away, but let us go toward

what is broken

Cuz what is the point of my words being spoken

If they are not provoking

you and provoking me

To go out into the darkness and see slaves set free

Cuz if not you and me, then who will go?

If we don't tell them, how will they know?

How will they see the light if the lights of the world don't glow?

Maybe we have got something wrong

Because church is not a building and worship is not a song

The church is not four walls

but a people ready to answer Jesus when he calls

And worship is not a melody and chords

But a life offered as a sacrifice to the Lord

An excerpt from "Worship," a spoken word poem by TEN20

CABIN FISH

I love to eat. God could have chosen any way for us to nourish our bodies, and it didn't have to be enjoyable. But in His great love and mercy, He chose food. Food is truly the center of our lives if you think about it. People work so they have money to buy food. At a very base level, life revolves around what we eat.

When asked about my favorite food, I always say cabin fish—it's just any fish we cook when at the cabin; there's no fish named cabin fish. There is something special about eating a fish you've caught, filleted, washed, battered, and fried yourself. Especially with my secret batter recipe —Bisquick plus whatever I can find in the spice cabinet. Peanut oil is the best for frying. Pan fried is best, but deep fried is more efficient. And efficiency is key when you need to feed about 15 people! Every time, we marvel at the number of fish we've caught and prepared. Without fail, someone always says, "There's no way we're gonna eat all this fish." And yet, in 27 years, I have never seen or heard of one leftover piece of fish.

Cabin fish wins as my favorite food because of sentimental value. But, I also enjoy steak, salmon, tacos and burritos (authentic please), chicken wings, tater tot hotdish (yes, in Minnesota, we call casserole a hotdish and duck, duck, goose we call duck, duck, grey duck), jerk chicken with red beans and rice, biscuits and gravy, hash brown pie (thanks, Amy), crepes (and Emma), chocolate chip pancakes, bacon (not too crispy), sausage (links or patties), fried plantains, spaghetti (my wife and I make the best in the family—sorry, everyone), cheeseburgers, fries, sweet potato fries, asparagus, broccoli, brussels sprouts, Totino's Pizza Rolls, all sugary cereals, chocolate chip cookies (pretty much all cookies), brownies, ice cream (not mint, chocolate, or java), mangos, raspberries, chicken fried rice, pad thai, eggrolls, wontons, sesame chicken, omelets, chicken wild rice soup, wild rice deviled eggs, yogurt, Ramen with Korean hot sauce, chocolate covered pretzels, and cookies (I know, I said it twice; I really like cookies).

> God could have chosen any way for us to nourish our bodies, and it didn't have to be enjoyable. But in His great love and mercy, He chose food. Food is truly the center of our lives if you think about it.

Hungry yet?

What are some of your favorite foods?

Some of us spend all day working to make money to buy food. We grab breakfast and run out the door. We meet someone for lunch to catch up or for business. We hope dinner is planned by the time we get home—or else there may be some serious *hanger*. Others spend all day prepping food and feeding the kids. Feed the kids, go to the store, feed the kids again, then start dinner. When we aren't eating, we are thinking about our next meal.

Food is the focus of life.
But not for Jesus.
Don't get me wrong, Jesus ate.

> *The Son of Man came eating and drinking, and you say, 'Here is a glutton and a drunkard, a friend of tax collectors and sinners'* (Luke 7:34).

For Jesus, life didn't revolve around food. For one, he went 40 days in a row without food! At that time, Satan played his card.

> *Then Jesus was led by the Spirit into the wilderness to be tempted by the devil. After fasting forty days and forty nights, he was hungry. The tempter came to him and said, "If you are the Son of God, tell these stones to become bread."*
>
> *Jesus answered, "It is written: 'Man shall not live on bread alone, but on every word that comes from the mouth of God'"* (Matthew 4:1–4).

Wow. Jesus compares God's Word to food. Why? In the same way that our bodies need food to survive, the very life of our souls is dependent upon consuming God's Word.

> Jesus compares God's Word to food. Why? In the same way that our bodies need food to survive, the very life of our souls is dependent upon consuming God's Word.

How often do we eat? How often do we think about food? How often does food influence our decisions—how we spend our time and money. How often do we gather with others around food?

Whatever your answer to all these questions, imagine if all your answers were also true about God's Word. According to Jesus, that's how it's supposed to be.

When I was in middle school, my dad decided to start a vineyard on land he'd bought in Wisconsin. My first job was on that vineyard. I remember writing "Vineyard Worker" on my resume when I applied for college—I'm sure that's what got me in. My dad paid $10 an hour, in cash. With two full days of work, I could buy myself a new baseball bat, hockey stick, or lots of candy.

One of our main jobs was to prune the vines. Grapevines grow into several branches. Some of these branches bear fruit and others don't. To continue growing, each branch takes nutrients from the soil. The first and most obvious step is to cut off the branches that aren't going to produce grapes—that way, they won't take nutrients from the branches that do produce.

You are now left with the grape-producing branches. From my very amateur understanding, you need to prune these branches to direct all the nutrients and energy to the best parts of the branches that will produce the most fruit.

Jesus said:

> *I am the true vine, and my Father is the gardener. He cuts off every branch in me that bears no fruit, while every branch that does bear fruit he prunes so that it will be even more fruitful. You are already clean because of the word I have spoken to you. Remain in me, as I also remain in you. No branch can bear fruit by itself; it must remain in the vine. Neither can you bear fruit unless you remain in me* (John 15:1–4).

If our souls are to have life as intended, Jesus is the vine we must connect ourselves to. If we don't, our souls will die—they will be cut off from the branch and thrown into the fire. I definitely don't want to be that branch.

But I want to do more than survive. I want my soul to thrive. I want to produce fruit in God's Kingdom so, one day, when I stand before Him, He will say:

> *'Well done, good and faithful servant! You have been faithful with a few things; I will put you in charge of many things. Come and share your master's happiness!'* (Matthew 25:21).

How about you? Do you want to bear fruit in God's Kingdom? Do you want your life to stand for something greater than yourself? Do you want to leave an eternal legacy behind you?

You need to stay connected to the vine.
You need to pray.
You need to read God's Word.
You need to fast—yes, from food, not just social media or Netflix.
You need to fellowship with other believers.
You need to confess your sins to others.
You need to exercise your faith.
You need to listen for the Holy Spirit.
You need to be obedient.
You need to abide.

Does this mean we earn our way to God? Absolutely not. It simply means that because He has saved us and filled us with the Holy Spirit, we have the great privilege of continually abiding in Him. The only place we will find true fulfillment in life is in abiding in Jesus.

> *Then Jesus declared, "I am the bread of life. Whoever comes to me will never go hungry, and whoever believes in me will never be thirsty* (John 6:35).

Food is amazing. But it is not meant to be the center of our lives—Jesus is.

Jesus' disciples once noticed that He hadn't eaten for a while:

> *Meanwhile his disciples urged him, "Rabbi, eat something." But he said to them, "I have food to eat that you know nothing about." Then his disciples said to each other, "Could someone have brought him food?" "My food," said Jesus, "is to do the will of him who sent me and to finish his work* (John 4:31–34).

Their minds were on food—Jesus' mind was on accomplishing God's will.

What is my mind on?

What is your mind on?

I want to get to the place where I see that my very spiritual life is completely dependent on continually abiding in the vine that is Jesus. Where I crave God's Word as much as I crave cookies!

The more we abide in Him, the more we will see how good He truly is, and the more we will want to abide.

Will you take this journey with me?

> *Taste and see that the Lord is good;*
>   *blessed is the one who takes refuge in him* (Psalm 34:8).

"Finding" Yourself

I had become a ministry leader, made amazing friends, met my future-wife, and began to grow in my faith exponentially. In addition to these formational experiences, there are a few moments that year that continue to stick out to me. All freshmen at Bethel University were required to take a class called Intro to Liberal Arts (ILA). ILA is a 1-credit class in which almost everyone earns an A. It is basically a course that helps to transition students to life at Bethel. As part of this class, we were required to read an article. I don't remember the name, author, or most of the content of this article, but I remember the main idea.

A common thought among young people is that they are "finding themselves." Go to college, move out, try new things, and *find yourself*; that is what our American culture tends to teach our youth. The author of the article came against this idea and said that we actually don't *find* ourselves, rather we *create* ourselves. The decisions we make, relationships we form, activities we get involved in, habits we develop and so on are all part of our formation. Even those who think they are just "finding themselves" are actually creating themselves; they just don't realize it.

> The decisions we make, relationships we form, activities we get involved in, habits we develop and so on are all part of our formation. Even those who think they are just "finding themselves" are actually creating themselves; they just don't realize it.

Ever since I read this article, I have been aware of this reality and aimed to apply it to my life. In college, I led multiple ministries, coached multiple sports, was involved in various Bible studies, played intramural sports, formed great relationships with friends and my future wife, and much more, all while maintaining a 4.0 GPA. Don't wait around to become the man or woman you want to be. Do it today; you never know what day will be your last.

Something Greater

As I read through the entire New Testament of the Bible over the course of my freshman year, I started to realize I had been to church my whole life, yet it seemed like I was hearing Jesus' words for the first time. Looking back, this is partially because I never paid attention in church. On the other hand, though, I actually *was* hearing His words for the first time.

I had only heard His words through a filter of comfortable, Americanized Christianity. In reality, Jesus' teachings are radical, and they call His followers into action. He taught that His followers must be willing to lose everything for the gospel, that anyone who wants to follow Him must pick up their cross *daily*. He taught that we are to love our enemies and care for the needy. He taught how fleeting and empty it is to acquire worldly possessions and be rich but not have a rich relationship with God.

> I had only heard His words through a filter of comfortable, Americanized Christianity. In reality, Jesus' teachings are radical, and they call His followers into action. He taught that His followers must be willing to lose everything for the gospel, that anyone who wants to follow Him must pick up their cross *daily*.

I distinctly remember having a conversation with Devin in which I first began to vocalize these thoughts. I asked him, "What makes us different from non-Christians?" The main difference I saw between professing Christian and non-Christian college students was that some of the Christians didn't drink, do drugs, or have sex. From what I read in the Bible, though, I was determined that as Christians, we should be defined by what we *do*, not just what we *don't do*.

It is not enough to just *not do* "bad" things. But are we doing the things that Jesus has called us to do? Are we making disciples, proclaiming the gospel, caring for the needy, taking up our crosses daily, etc.? It was these types of thoughts and questions that began to change my life. They drove me to live for something greater than myself—to live for Jesus.

KOINONIA

That Spring I decided to apply to be on the "Welcome Week" team. Welcome Week is the first week that students are on campus. And as you may have guessed, the Welcome Week team is responsible for *welcoming* new students. The Welcome Week team consisted of several committees, and each planned the different events that make up Welcome Week. Even though it was not my first choice, I was placed on the Spiritual Committee. In addition to the duties of the team as a whole, each committee had one or two big responsibilities. For the Spiritual Committee, this big responsibility was an event known as *Koinonia*. *Koinonia* is a Greek word that describes the fellowship of the people of God. *Koinonia* is a major event that takes place annually, consisting of worship music, personal faith testimonies, and a message from the campus pastor. It is the culmination of Welcome Week.

One of the duties in planning *Koinonia* was to find three students to share their personal testimony at the event. I remember sitting in the crowd as a freshman and hearing an upperclassman give his testimony; I was very inspired. I had never heard anyone speak so openly about his past to such a large crowd. Hearing his story of transformation through Christ made me want to grow closer to God and be able to share my story like he had.

As we looked for students, we wanted to find testimonies that aligned with the theme of the event: releasing your burdens. The more I thought about this theme, the more I realized that my own story of encountering Christ was a good fit. It was when I first confessed my sin that my burdens had been lifted. In one of our committee meetings, I suggested that I could be a candidate to share my story. The committee agreed to keep me in mind as an option.

That night, as I lay in bed, I pictured myself sharing my testimony in front of a crowd of more than 1,000 people and wondered what exactly I would say. I had never really vocalized my faith journey at that point. Earlier that week, my good friend Andrew O'Reilly, aka AO, had introduced me to spoken word poetry. He showed me a video by Jefferson Bethke called *Why I Hate Religion, But Love Jesus*. This video rocked my world. It embodied hip-hop, culture, lyricism, and most of all, it pointed people to Jesus.

I had never written any lyrics or done anything creative or musical in my life, but as I lay awake thinking of what I would say, this thought entered my mind: *What if you did spoken word poetry?* I laughed to myself and thought, *No way, I could never do something like that.* All of a sudden, the lines started coming to me one-by-one. I heard a voice in my head saying, *Get up and write this down.* I had no desire to get out of bed; I had a chemistry lab at 7:30 the next morning and had stayed up way too late talking to Abigail. However, I felt a burning sensation in my chest and couldn't sleep, so I got up and typed out my first spoken word poem.

During our next spiritual committee meeting, I shared my spoken word poem with the rest of the committee. They were amazed. It was decided unanimously that I would be one of the speakers at *Koinonia*. Sharing this poem at *Koinonia* was one of the most powerful moments of my life. I had never felt so close to God; it felt as if His very Spirit was speaking through me.

When I finished, the 1,500-member crowd erupted in standing ovation. People I didn't know came up to me after the event with tears in their eyes, thanking me and giving me hugs. It was unlike anything I had ever experienced. Pastor Laurel Bunker, the campus pastor, gave me several shoutouts in her closing sermon. For the weeks following, people would see me around campus and say things like, "Thank you so much for sharing your story; it was truly amazing." I figured that God had given me a one-time spoken word message for that particular moment. Little did I know, that was just the beginning.

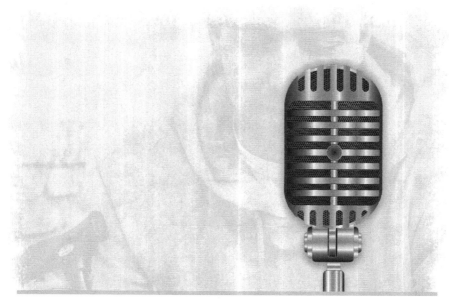

CHAPTER 8

TRAINING GROUNDS

Then Jesus came to them and said, "All authority in heaven and on earth has been given to me. Therefore go and make disciples of all nations, baptizing them in the name of the Father and of the Son and of the Holy Spirit, and teaching them to obey everything I have commanded you. And surely I am with you always, to the very end of the age."

— Matthew 28:18–20

What if there was a disease that covered the earth?
A disease that everyone had from birth
A disease infected all of humanity
Causing each person to lose their sanity
And what if the disease were fatal?
And we weren't able
To stop it

All we could do is watch it

Destroy the world day by day

And leave a trail of destruction on its way

And what if this was a disease that X-rays don't show?

So the fact that they have it, most people don't even know

But what if you were to know

That there is a cure?

That you didn't have to live in fear

That with just one dose of this vaccine

You could instantly be permanently clean

Of course you would take it you wouldn't think twice

In fact in order to get it, you'd probably pay any price

And not only that but you have been given an infinite amount

Is this something you would want people to know about?

Would you shout it

From the top of a mountain?

Would you give it to as many people as you could?

Whether they lived in the country, suburbs or the hood

If they were on earth it

Would be worth it

To save them from death

You would spread this vaccine until your very last breath

And it wouldn't matter who they were

Because they all have the disease and they all need the cure

Would your mission be ended

If someone got offended?

Thinking they didn't have the infection

Or would you be held back by the fear of rejection?

Or would you be too in love with your comfortable life?

Too busy with your kids and your wife

And take all your time and keep if for yourself

Well the cure to the disease just sits on your shelf

No! You would go to any length

To spread this cure with all your strength
You would do anything to spread this cure
Right? The answer seems obvious but are you sure?
Because the truth is this disease is real. It's called sin
It is the disease that everyone has deep within
It has infected each and every person
It has caused the perversion
In our society
It's why we have rioting
It's why there is sickness
And wickedness
It's why there is murder
It's why her dad hurt her
It's why there are sex slaves
And labor slaves
And late night raves
Where a girl in good shape
Gets a pill in her drink and it turns into a rape
It's why people die of starvation
And get whipped on plantations
And have no clean water
And their village gets slaughtered
It's the cause of violent repression
And oppression
And depression
It causes civil war
Guerrilla war
World war
And so much more
But most of all, it causes us to lose sight of what we were made for
To walk in a perfect relationship with our Creator
And instead walk in a fear of dying
And a life of trying

To fulfill ourselves with what we can buy

That cute girl or guy

What kind of car we drive

We try and try to feel alive

With alcohol and drugs

Or bicep curls and shrugs

Or looking at porn

But we always end up torn

Inside

Because no matter what we try, we never end up satisfied

And there is always something more

So you need just one more pour

And you need one more hit

And to get a little more fit

And get a little less fat

But even after that

You won't quite feel happy

And you will still feel crappy

Until you get that next thing you just have to have it

Can't you see this is a never ending cycle we just have to quit?

So as you can see, this disease is not a superstition

But the good news is that the cure is also non-fiction

Because one man in history lived without the infection

And through his death on the cross and resurrection

His innocent blood offers us correction

To be forgiven and restored back to perfection

And for us and God to have a complete connection

Sealed forever through the Holy Spirit's protection

But what needs to happen first is an insurrection

Where the government of your heart is overthrown

And you see that your life is no longer your own

Because you have been shown

Such great love that you give Jesus your heart's throne

And once you do, you enter the Kingdom

And you don't have to live in sin, because you can live in freedom

So let me ask you the question that I earlier:

Will you spread this love? Would you spread this cure?

Jesus said to let your light shine before others even if they are jerks

Jesus said to let your light shine before others even when it hurts

So that they will see your good works

And give glory to God

To not do this would be so odd

He said to preach the good news to all of creation

That is a pretty obvious call regardless of your interpretation

So if you believe in this cure it's time to stop living in stillness

Cuz people are walking around with a deadly illness

And you have been entrusted with the medication

So don't hold it back but let others receive this salvation

Heal the sick, raise the dead, cast out demons, pray God would send out laborers

Make disciples of all nations, as you love yourself so love your neighbors

Let the deaf hear let the blind be seeing

This call is amazing and worth every ounce of our being

So rise up church, it's time to take back what's been lost

For Jesus said to follow Him you'd have to pick up your cross

"The Cure," a spoken word poem by TEN20

https://www.youtube.com/watch?v=iOV6oCSLkLU

TIGHTROPE

I once heard a story of a great tightrope walker. He walked across canyons and between skyscrapers on a tightrope while carrying his assistant on his back. Multitudes would gather to observe this daredevil and cheer him on. "Do you believe?" he would shout. He was met with booming applause and hoorays from the onlookers. "Do you believe I can walk across this rope with my assistant on my back?" The same response from the crowd followed. He would then ask one more question:

"Will one of *you* let me carry you on my back across this rope?"

Crickets.

Time and time again, no brave volunteer stepped forward. The stuntman would pick his assistant up and give him a piggyback ride across the tightrope.

Many people say they believe in God and in Jesus. They call themselves Christians. But what about when Jesus calls us to get on His back as He walks across the tightrope? What about putting our life in His hands? What about trusting Him with our time, finances, families, fulfillment, and even our safety?

I don't say this to look down on anyone, but I have known and observed many people who are like the members of the tightrope walker's crowd. They go to church on Christmas, Easter, and maybe even every Sunday. But that is it. Their life has nothing to do with Jesus outside of church. Imagine how exciting it was for the tightrope walker's assistant. Crossing canyons, knowing he would reach the other side safely. Jesus calls us to an adventure. It is fulfilling, invigorating, and sometimes even frightful, but we know He will never let go of us. To join Him on the adventure, though, we have to trust Him with everything.

I would soon get a better picture of what trusting Jesus actually looks like.

HOW COULD I SAY NO?

Food, transportation, basketball, dodgeball, broomball, friends, and more. Just $25. It was a college student's dream come true. *How could I say no?* This was the invitation I received to attend a winter retreat with one of the on-campus ministries at Bethel. My friends and I decided to sign up, and the next thing we knew, we were in a 12-passenger van headed to Camp Shamineau. Not only did we have an amazing time playing games, eating food, and building friendships, but we also heard a clearly articulated gospel message by a captivating speaker.

Up to that point, I knew I had encountered Jesus and that God loved me. I had been reading the Bible, praying, and growing in my faith. When I heard the speaker share the gospel, however, I gained a new understanding of my sin, God's grace, Jesus' death and the cross and His resurrection, and God's call and purpose for my life. That weekend was not only super fun, but it also left me with an even greater desire to study the Bible and share the love of Christ.

On that winter retreat, my friends and I got to know two of the leaders. One was a junior at Bethel and had been involved in the campus ministry for a few years. The other was on staff, but we didn't know much about him. He seemed like a cool guy, was a good athlete, and loved Jesus. These two leaders became in college what Theis, Nels and Moberg were to me in high school. They were intentional and consistently invited us guys to eat, play sports, and read the Bible together.

> Jesus calls us to an adventure. It is fulfilling, invigorating, and sometimes even frightful, but we know He will never let go of us. To join Him on the adventure, though, we have to trust Him with everything.

One day, our leader told a few of us about an opportunity to go on a spring break missions trip. A hurricane had hit New York, so we would be helping a local church with providing relief for those impacted. Again, food, transportation, and lodging were all covered; all we had to pay was $100. Sure enough, before we knew it, Nathaniel Van Loon, Jake Toedter and I were off to New York, this time in a 15-passenger van.

THE BIG APPLE

Our trip leader was Josh Schrock. We knew nothing about him either, except for the same things we knew about our other leaders. Our first day in New York, he woke everyone up early. I figured it was time for breakfast or time to meet people from the church. Nope. It was time to read the Bible and pray. Josh made sure we got up every morning and studied the Bible before we did anything else. He was the first person I had spent time with who lived in such a way. He sought every opportunity to share the love of Christ with everyone he encountered. I even witnessed him meet a young man, give him his very own Bible, give him a ride home, and bring groceries to his house, which he bought with his own money.

This week in New York with Josh was the first time I had an extended, up-close look at someone who was totally sold out for Christ. It was awesome and inspiring, and it made me want to follow Josh's example since it was evident that he was following the example of Jesus.

DECISIONS

Our leaders kept telling us guys about some great summer program that was put on by the campus ministry. It was a two-month-long trip to South Carolina where students from four different colleges all lived together in a motel. We would all work at Walmart together, study the Bible, share the gospel, and grow in our faith journeys; we even had the choice to join the Athletes in Training (AIT) program and work out together almost every day. The staff said I could join, even though I didn't play a college sport since the rest of my friends were football players.

I had grown up with a love for lyricism and flow, but when I first started following Christ, I didn't know that Jesus and hip-hop were compatible.

This seemed like an awesome opportunity, but it wasn't my only option that summer. Devin's RA invited him to apply as a camp counselor at a Christian camp; there were two open positions, and Devin invited me to apply as well. I applied and interviewed for the camp counselor position but wasn't sure what I wanted to do. I prayed that God would open one door and close the other. Sure enough, I was not selected for the camp counselor position, so that summer I headed down to Myrtle Beach.

MYRTLE BEACH

The summer program was, for the most part, an amazing experience. Every morning we woke up before work to study the Bible together. Everyone studied the same few verses each morning, which made for great conversation as we spent our days working at Walmart. After work, the athletes and I headed to the gym to lift weights, run sprints, and practice football. In the evenings, we heard from a speaker about the different aspects of Christian life—sharing the gospel, living in community, managing money, relationships, and more.

On the weekends, we hit Myrtle Beach and shared the good news of Jesus with anyone who would listen. In our free time, we played Spikeball, cook, do laundry, or swim. That summer I became close friends with Nathaniel Van Loon, Jake Toedter, and Andrew O'Reilly; the three of them ended up being groomsmen in my wedding, and we remain close to this day. Besides growing deeper in my faith, building awesome friendships, and having tons of fun, three things from that summer really stuck with me.

HIP-HOP AND JESUS?

Christian hip-hop was the soundtrack to the summer program. The only Christian rap I ever heard before college was a couple of songs by Lecrae. I had grown up with a love for lyricism and flow, but when I first started following Christ, I didn't know that Jesus and hip-hop were compatible. In addition to being introduced to spoken word poetry by AO, Nathaniel had introduced me to the world of CHH (Christian hip-hop). His dad was a pastor, so CHH was the only rap he was allowed to listen to. I first downloaded Spotify when I was in college, and Nathaniel created a playlist for me with all the best Christian rappers. I instantly fell in love with the music of Lecrae, Andy Mineo, Trip Lee, and KB. Before KB blew up, I got to see him in concert at Bethel with only about 30 people in the crowd.

I fell more and more in love with CHH that summer and wrote my second spoken word poem. Over the two months in SC, we studied the Book of Galatians. I took everything I had learned and summarized it into poetry. I ended up sharing this poem in front of everyone at a big event and got a lot of great feedback. I started to wonder if maybe God had given me this gift as a way to talk about Him creatively.

MORE RUSTINESS

The Athletes In Training workouts were no joke. I had worked out consistently during my freshman year, but not as hard or as seriously as at AIT. When we started lifting heavier weights, my friends would joke about how I shook as I lifted. I also had trouble balancing during some of the exercises, like one-legged squats and step ups. I figured I was just rusty since I hadn't worked out seriously in a year. I was also having more trouble than usual on the field. Nathaniel and AO were both kickers, and I was the one who caught their kicks. I was having trouble tracking and catching kicks, even though I had been a kick returner in middle and high school football. I was also having trouble catching passes on the run and throwing the ball well.

Beyond my poor performance on the field, I was feeling extremely fatigued; some days while driving from Walmart to AIT, I would nearly fall asleep at the wheel. I continued coming up with reasons for the ways I was feeling.

Well, if you don't use it, you lose it. I must be rusty. Plus, we were getting up early and working all day, so it made sense how tired I was. Not to mention, I shared a double bed with my roommate, and I faced the ever-present threat of waking up to a cockroach crawling on my body. I was still more athletic than most of the others in our group, so I didn't think anything was wrong with me. I continued explaining away my fatigue and my decrease in athletic ability, and I tried not to think about it too much.

AN OPEN CANVAS

On one of the last nights in SC, we had the privilege of hearing from the same speaker who had spoken at the winter retreat. He asked a simple question that forever changed my life. He asked, "Are you a picture book or an open canvas?" A picture book, he explained, was like drawing out several pictures of what you want your life to look like and inviting God to join you on this journey. An open canvas, on the other hand, meant you simply give God the paint brush and let Him go to work.

> I didn't think anything was wrong with me. I continued explaining away my fatigue and my decrease in athletic ability, and I tried not to think about it too much.

I realized in that moment I was a picture book. I had planned out my life and invited God to join me. I was studying biology on a pre-med track. Why? Was I passionate about the medical field? No. Did I enjoy science? Not particularly. But my dad, grandpa, two uncles, one cousin, and sister were all doctors. School came naturally to me, so I figured I might as well be a doctor too. I thought it would be nice to help people, make a lot of money, and have the status and recognition that comes along with having "Dr." before your name. At that moment, I decided to surrender my future plans to God.

I wanted to be an open canvas.

How about you?

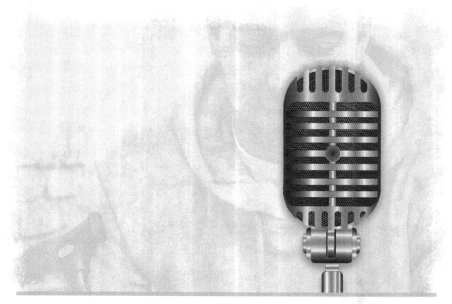

CHAPTER 9

UNA ADVENTURA

"Blessed are the poor in spirit, for theirs is the kingdom of heaven. Blessed are those who mourn, for they will be comforted. Blessed are the meek, for they will inherit the earth. Blessed are those who hunger and thirst for righteousness, for they will be filled. Blessed are the merciful, for they will be shown mercy. Blessed are the pure in heart, for they will see God. Blessed are the peacemakers, for they will be called children of God. Blessed are those who are persecuted because of righteousness, for theirs is the kingdom of heaven."

— Matthew 5:3–10

He is cyclical
He breaks families
He breaks homes
He is self-perpetuating
He is the rumbling in the stomach of a child who goes to bed hungry

He is the inability to access the 5 cent treatments of the diseases that take millions of lives each year

You can't escape him

He clutches on to you and crushes your hopes and dreams

He doesn't rest

He is always working for the enemy.

If your not careful you will subconsciously slip into his trap and be stuck for good

He is Poverty

They say he can be shocking in certain faraway places like third world countries

Or the cities surrounded by nice suburban neighborhoods in which we live

And I found that to some extent they were correct as I ventured to Guatemala and I saw him first hand

He had taken the form of dirt floors and metal sheet walls

He looked like empty cupboards and children selling souvenirs in the streets to rich folks like me rather than being educated

But to my surprise, where he was most prevalent, I met someone else

This was someone that I had seen before

We had only met briefly in passing

But here

We truly got to know each other

He didn't mind inviting me into his home even though he couldn't even afford his daughter's education

He wanted to bless me with a feast even if he didn't know if he would make enough money tomorrow to feed himself

He worshipped God truly

With a pure heart

With joy and childlike faith

His name is Love

I had never gazed with him face to face as clearly as I did when poverty was in the very same room with us

And it is true that Poverty shocked me as I went, but the one who truly shocked me was Love

And even more shocking than my arrival in Guatemala was my return home

If you can even call it home, my encounter with Love had me questioning where my home truly is

And as I made my way into the Miami airport, I was reacquainted with old acquaintances

Hurry, Selfish Ambition, and Emptiness were all there to greet me at the door

As I live in America now, where Poverty, well he can easily be ignored

And Love, he seldom comes around anymore

I can't help but wonder, who is really poor?

"Poverty," a spoken word poem by TEN20

SPRING BREAK

When I was a sophomore in high school, my family decided to do something different. Ever since I can remember, my family took warm-weather vacations every year for spring break. We went to Florida almost every year, except for the year we went to Jamaica and the year we went to Italy. In 2010, we decided instead to take a service trip to Guatemala. The plan was to help a local orphanage build one of their buildings, which we did. This was my first encounter with poverty. Homes consisted of tin walls screwed together over dirt floors. I had never seen anything like it.

As with most typical short-term service or mission trips, we spent one day as tourists; our destination was Antigua, the most popular tourist destination in Guatemala. It's modernized but has an old Spanish look

I saw young children spending all day trying to sell souvenirs to tourists rather than getting an education. Many families weren't even sure if they could afford their next meal let alone school fees and uniforms.

that attracts many sightseers. Though the architecture of Antigua is beautiful, I noticed something not so beautiful happening in the city. I saw young children spending all day trying to sell souvenirs to tourists rather than getting an education. Many families weren't even sure if they could afford their next meal let alone school fees and uniforms.

Seeing poverty up close did two things for me as a 16-year-old. On one hand, it broke my heart. I couldn't believe that people lived in such conditions when all my friends and I lived in big houses and drove cars to school. It didn't make sense that some people can be so rich while others are so poor. Even at age 16, I knew the disparity and injustice wasn't right. I started to connect more with the idea that my life had a purpose beyond playing sports and getting girls to go out with me.

On the other hand, it made me realize how privileged I was. I had the opportunity to get an education while other kids sold trinkets and shined shoes in the streets, hoping to make enough money to eat that night. Up until that point, I had not taken my education very seriously; I did pretty well but by no means had straight A's. Since getting back from Guatemala, I have earned straight A's in every course—aside from the A- in A.P. Government during my senior slide—including all courses during college and now my Master's degree, which I'm one semester away from earning.

We should make the most of every opportunity we have. Not only do others not have the same opportunities, but when we truly make the most of them, we end up in a place where we can help others.

No-Brainer

I was thrilled to find out that Bethel offered a semester-long study abroad program in Guatemala. I always liked my high school Spanish classes and was able to communicate decently my first time in Guatemala, so I decided I would earn a minor in Spanish. This study abroad was the perfect combination. Half our time would be spent living in Antigua taking classes; the other half would be spent living with a host family in a more rural area and doing community service. Signing up was a no-brainer.

> It made me realize how privileged I was. I had the opportunity to get an education while other kids sold trinkets and shined shoes in the streets, hoping to make enough money to eat that night.

There were several options for what type of community service we wanted to do—everything from social work to agriculture. I was still on the pre-med track at the time, so I decided I would serve in a doctor's office, even though I was questioning whether or not the medical field was right for me. As the trip approached, I prayed that God would start to reveal His desire for my career and my future.

Being back in Guatemala was amazing. Nathaniel was also a Spanish minor, so we signed up together and were roommates. The landscape of mountains, lakes, and volcanoes was beautiful, but the most beautiful part of Guatemala by far was the people. It is difficult to get to know people in just one week, though I did get to meet some awesome people the first time I went. This time, I was there for four months and truly got to experience life in Guatemala.

Our first week was spent in Magdalena where we did community service and stayed with a host family. Nathaniel and I quickly befriended our host family and had an amazing time with them, sharing meals and stories in mediocre-level Spanish. My days were spent in the clinic taking temperatures, blood pressure, and washing prescription bottles. Though I enjoyed my time in the clinic, I was wondering more and more whether or not the medical field was for me. At the end of the week, we left for Antigua where we would spend the next two months.

"Estábamos Jugando"

I may be biased since Nathaniel is one of my best friends, but I truly believe he could have been an NFL kicker. Before we started attending Bethel University, its football team had a rocky reputation for making extra points, let alone field goals. Nathaniel could do both with ease; he was pretty much automatic. Sadly, early in his sophomore season, an opposing lineman landed on Nathaniel's planted leg after an extra point, tearing his ACL, MCL, and meniscus. Nathaniel had planned to rehab while in Guatemala, so he'd brought along a few exercise bands to do so.

On one of our first days in Antigua, Nathaniel, our other roommate, and I were engaged in a heartfelt conversation. We had started getting to know our third roommate better, and we were talking on a deeper level about our personal faith journeys and what we felt God calling us to do in life. The conversation shifted toward missions and working to eradicate poverty. Our hearts were in the right place, but our maturity hadn't quite caught up. Somehow, we came up with an idea.

"What if we were slingshot missionaries?"

"What do you mean?" The others hadn't yet caught onto my vision.

"We could go around and slingshot Bibles and food to people." I had painted the picture perfectly. I'm not sure if you have been around a group of young men, but when they get their minds set on something, it's difficult to stop them. In such moments, all logic goes out the window.

"Let's see if it works." I grabbed one of Nathaniel's resistance bands off the floor and his Bible from his bed. I instructed the others each to hold one side of the band. They mindlessly followed my instructions. Setting the Bible in the middle, one hand above the band, one hand below, I began to pull back.

As I was letting go, I snapped back into reality. I realized we were new guests in a host home and that our makeshift slingshot was aimed directly at our bedroom window. At that point, it was too late. The window completely shattered directly into the dining area. After ceasing to laugh hysterically, we started to plot how we were going to explain this situation to our host family. We quickly realized that none of us had a sufficient Spanish vocabulary to explain what happened. We eventually told our hosts, "estábamos jugando" (we were playing). To this day, I wonder what they imagine to have happened.

This is more so just a funny story, but there is a point. When we smashed the window with a Bible slingshot, our hearts were in the right place. Our actions, however, were a bit misguided. It is good to have zeal, but zeal must be exercised in a well thought out manner. You will see in this chapter that I had a lot of zeal for what my future would look like. I am thankful for the people who have counseled me with godly wisdom and taught me to slow down and think before acting.

A MAJOR CHANGE

In Antigua we stayed with an elderly woman who had two maids. We spent weekdays going to school, going to the gym, doing homework, eating with our host family, and having group events in the evenings. We spent weekends taking excursions, going to church, and exploring the city. Nathaniel and I got over the window road bump with our hosts and soon began to develop great relationships with Doña Cristi, Maria, and Juanita. I continued praying daily for God to reveal His plan for me and let me know if I should change my major.

It was common for Americans to get sick in Guatemala and, eventually, I succumbed to the inevitable. However, unlike most stomach illnesses we Americans tend to contract, mine didn't start getting better after a few days, instead it grew much worse. I ended up bed-ridden for about two weeks. I had a fever, chills, dizziness, fatigue, vomiting, and diarrhea. Sharing a bathroom and having explosive diarrhea led to some unfortunate encounters with the maid in the bathroom. I'll leave it at that. My classmates, girlfriend, and relatives were very worried about me. With no TV or internet, there wasn't much to do all day—when I wasn't in the bathroom or asleep—besides read the Bible and pray. All the days blended together, and I began to feel like I was only half alive. I wondered if I would ever get better. Looking back now,

God had something to tell me, and this seemed to be the only way I would stop and listen.

One day while reading, I came across Proverbs 15:16–17: "Better a little with the fear of the Lord than great wealth with turmoil. Better a small serving of vegetables with love than a fattened calf with hatred." Something in me clicked. These verses put words to what God had been teaching my heart. From a worldly standpoint, I was seeing people who had very little but had greater joy than many of the wealthy people I knew back home. I met people like Marcos, who didn't have many earthly possessions, yet he possessed God's purpose for his life—working daily with youth in the community to teach sports and feed them both physically and spiritually. I began to see the truth of the beatitudes (Matthew 5:3–11) while simultaneously seeing the emptiness of materialism.

Proverbs 15:16–17: "Better a little with the fear of the Lord than great wealth with turmoil. Better a small serving of vegetables with love than a fattened calf with hatred."

My worldview was turning upside down.

This seemed to be the answer to my question: God wanted me to be an overseas missionary. I loved what I was feeling in Guatemala and wanted to feel it the rest of my life. In my zeal, I came up with what seemed like a genius plan: drop out of college, marry Abbie, and head overseas into the mission field. *Genius, right?* Apparently not. I forgot to factor into my plan that Abigail also had a life, commitments, hopes, and dreams. As you may have guessed, she shut down my plan, but not completely. She actually was on board with getting married and becoming missionaries; she just wanted to graduate college first.

When I regained my strength, I contacted my college advisor and changed my major to Teaching English as a Second Language (TESL). I figured if I was going to finish, then I might as well prepare myself for the mission field; TESL could take me all over the world in addition to providing me with a teaching license at home in case we needed to be in the states for any reason. When we went back to Magdalena for the last six weeks of our trip, my community service site changed from the clinic to teaching English at an elementary school. I had so much fun and was convinced I had made the right choice, even though I enjoyed recess much more than my English lessons. I have so many great memories in Guatemala and will forever cherish my time there. I have since been back twice and hope to return again. It is a beautiful country with amazing people, and it taught me what is truly important in life.

JUST TO CLARIFY...

I want to end this chapter with a clarification. I want to make it clear that there is nothing sexy about poverty. Yes, my worldview changed in Guatemala. Yes, I met people who were poor but possessed great spiritual riches. However, it is too easy for those of us who live in more developed countries to end the conversation there. We can think that poor people are happy and, therefore, we don't need to do anything to eradicate poverty. Poverty is devastating. Countless people lose their lives daily because they lack access to substantial food, clean water, and proper medication. We all play a role in the wealth dynamics of this world. My prayer is we would all seek practical ways to meet basic human needs and uphold the dignity of all people everywhere.

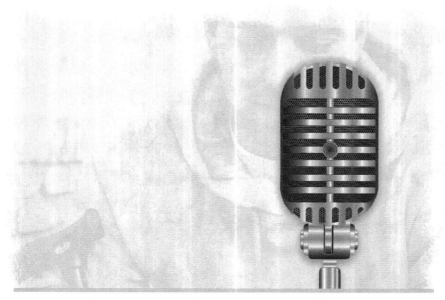

CHAPTER 10

REAL MEN

He has shown you, O mortal, what is good. And what does the Lord require of you? To act justly and to love mercy and to walk humbly with your God.

— Micah 6:8

I have a question for you: what if your whole life you have seen the world through a broken lens?

See everything depends on your perspective

And what if the truth you were taught by your collective context is no truth at all?

What if you have been taught lies by society?

Open your eyes for me

And see

But first I'm asking you to become blind

Forget everything you have ever known, rewind

To when you were just a child and had an open mind

No culturally ingrained blinders are permitted

Childhood, let's revisit

Think about it. In school we're taught that in 1492

Columbus sailed the ocean blue

And discovered America. Like he discovered America? Like there weren't people already living there, and he's some kind of hero.

Like it's healthy

And there is zero

Problem with the fact that he enslaved human beings to be wealthy

And to have gold

No, that is not the story that we have been told

And thanksgiving, we celebrate a nice meal shared with the Indians and pilgrims

Like there were no victims

Like there was no genocide against natives

Like it was a nice creative plan

To strip the land out of their hands

And force their remnant onto reservations

Like they weren't mistreated

And all the treaties were completed

Maybe the truth has been hidden from us

Like in history class

We learn that injustice towards Blacks

Is a thing of the past

We don't learn about racial profiling

Or that police can be overly violent

No, these matters are kept silent

But think about it, try it

In science

You learn that the genius woven into each blood cell that miraculously flows through our veins

Is the result of a Big Bang

Like the creation doesn't need a creator

As if a tent doesn't need a tentmaker

In all other fields we don't apply that logic

But you're willing to wager eternity on it?

I have a problem with that

In fact

Maybe you grew up believing the opposite, and it's possible

That you even went to church and learned the American half-gospel

Where you pray a prayer to get to heaven

And go to church and learn from the reverend

But you've never been changed

Cuz you have no relationship with God the other six days

And the red letters in your Bible seem so strange

Cuz what you're taught is so far from what he's actually saying

You never learned that Jesus actually got off the cross and out of the grave and gave His spirit to those who live in repentance

Knowing we deserve a death sentence

But instead it's

Grace and mercy and love

And you never learned the book of Acts

Where faith took action and actually impacted the population

And it wasn't safe then

But they had no fear

Knowing that if they died here

They would enter into eternal life

And the same man who denied the name three times for the same name would be crucified

And we are called to be of like mind

Picking up our cross daily

Not afraid to die for the name we

Proclaim plainly

And boldly

No we

May not have heard that in church

So I have a question for you: what if your whole life you have seen the world through a broken lens?

See everything depends on your perspective

And what if the truth you were taught by your collective context is no truth at all?

What if you have been taught lies by society?

Open your eyes for me

And see

That the good news is that God's love for you and me

Is displayed by his son dying on a tree

So come home, and believe

And be free.

"Broken Lens," a spoken word poem by TEN20

https://www.youtube.com/watch?v=ZTnktjXj2FE

BACK TO REALITY

Coming off the plane ride from Guatemala City into the Miami airport was like waking up from a good dream. Guatemala is by no means a perfect place, but the Guatemalan culture is one that values people over schedules. If you saw someone you knew while on your way to an event, you would be late to that event because you would stay and talk to your friend. When you finally showed up, no one would be mad; they probably showed up late too. During the afternoons in Magdalena, everything would shut down for 1–2 hours, so people could eat lunch, rest, and socialize. Such a thing would never happen in the US—business owners wouldn't be able to stand missing out on profits. Even Chick-Fil-A closing on Sundays is an anomaly. I had grown to love this way of life that valued relationships over consumerism, materialism, and individualism. The hustle and bustle of the Miami airport was the pinch that woke me up and brought me back to reality.

I was in culture shock. The images of dirt floors and tin walls were fresh in my mind as I drove through the suburb I grew up in. I couldn't observe the big houses, giant yards, and abundance of food and money without thinking of the children selling souvenirs on the streets of Guatemala. On one of my first nights back in the US, Abigail and I attended the groom's dinner of a couple we knew. I was deeply disturbed by the excess of food and drinks coupled with the fancy venue adorned with expensive decorations. I couldn't relax and enjoy myself. Abigail kept asking me what was wrong, but I couldn't articulate what I was feeling and experiencing.

> The images of dirt floors and tin walls were fresh in my mind as I drove through the suburb I grew up in. I couldn't observe the big houses, giant yards, and abundance of food and money without thinking of the children selling souvenirs on the streets of Guatemala.

In Guatemala, my eyes had been opened to injustice. I took classes on the history of the country. I learned in detail about colonialism, oligarchical power, and even the US military involvement that led to years of civil war and genocide against indigenous people. I learned how Guatemala's past impacted the present and why 98% of the land was owned by 2% of the people. I saw firsthand the impacts of past injustices. Little did I know, I was soon going to see similar realities back home.

GARBAGE BALL

Wayne Andersen is the father of one of my high school friends. Wayne and I knew of each other but didn't really know each other well. That summer, some of my high school friends who were home from college invited me to check out Real Men. Wayne had started Real Men after working as a disciplinary paraprofessional at a local middle school that was very culturally diverse. Wayne soon figured out that the same handful of guys got in trouble again and again. Many of these guys had somewhat similar situations; poverty and fatherlessness were two of the main common denominators. Wayne saw a deeper need than what he could offer in the public school setting. He saw that these young men needed male biblical mentorship, and thus, Real Men was born. When I first showed up, Real Men consisted of Thursday night meetings in which we ate, had Bible study, and played garbage ball—basketball with garbage cans substituting as hoops. When we were done, I would give some of the boys a ride home.

ONE TOWN, TWO WORLDS

Rides home were truly an eye-opening experience. Most of the young men I drove home lived in low-income apartments. Until then, almost every family I'd been acquainted with owned a home. I thought of apartments as being for college students, single corporate workers, and Indian families—the only apartments in my neighborhood were predominantly Indian-occupied. The middle school that Wayne worked at is in the same school district that I grew up in. When I first started showing up there, I was surprised to see how diverse it was. There had been only a handful of people of color at my middle school—which was in the same district.

The more I got to know these guys and their stories, I started to wonder how it was possible that we could attend school in the same district but live in two entirely different worlds.

Almost every young man who attended Real Men was Black. The more I got to know these guys and their stories, I started to wonder how it was possible that we could attend school in the same district but live in two entirely different worlds. All my friends lived in big houses. Our parents had well-paying jobs. We drove nice cars. We had a high-quality education and a plethora of top-notch extra-curricular activities readily available to us. This didn't seem to be the case for the members of Real Men.

The middle and high school that I attended was predominantly White and consistently performed at the top of the state in both academics and athletics. The middle school that the Real Men members went to fed the other high school in the district. This school is very diverse and tends to perform lower than my alma mater both academically and athletically. Both schools are in the same district. I began wondering how this was possible and why things were the way they were.

I began to learn of the history of our country in a new light. I had previously been taught about Thanksgiving and Martin Luther King, Jr. giving a speech that ended racism. I was now learning about Native American boarding schools, mass incarceration, red-lining and much more. As I had seen in Guatemala, I began seeing how a history of injustice had impacted the present in our nation. I resolved then that I would aim to be an agent of reconciliation. I am still learning daily what that means and how I can live it out, and I hope that I can encourage others to do the same.

All this is from God, who reconciled us to himself through Christ and gave us the ministry of reconciliation: (2 Corinthians 5:18).

Real Men eventually graduated from garbage ball into a real gym, which is just one example of how the ministry grew. Eventually, we had female leaders and students, and so it could no longer be called Real Men. The name *Quincy* was chosen after buying a house on Quincy Street where we began holding our meetings. The young men of Quincy turned into a family. In a given week, we'd have our Bible study and meal on Thursday, basketball practice on Friday (after which guys would sometimes spend the night at my college house), a basketball game on Saturday, and church on Sunday with brunch afterwards. Then we would do the same thing the following week.

When I was serving with Quincy, I felt I was doing what I was meant to do. I was also writing and performing spoken word poetry more regularly and had started to be seen as a legitimate artist. I knew God was calling me to be a missionary, but I started wondering if He was really calling me overseas; I felt that maybe He was calling me to my own backyard.

CHAPTER 11

WHAT DO YOU WANT TO BE WHEN YOU GROW UP?

For we are God's handiwork, created in Christ Jesus to do good works, which God prepared in advance for us to do.

— Ephesians 2:10

Dear school kids
Especially the cool kids
And the, I wanna break every rule, kids
First of all, I'm sorry
Us educators act like we never make mistakes
We have been fake
So no more deception
First off I don't like sitting through a lecture

So I don't know why I expect your
Attention
So I don't blame you for sleeping and snoring
I mean if I'm honest, school is boring
You seem surprised
Maybe you students have never realized
That we too are human beings
And I don't like the fact that after being
Here all day I have to bring work home
So why would I assign homework?
Like doing assignments at home works...
When I don't get it
Should I ask my parents?
What if mom's on a drug and can't quit it
What if dad never got acquitted
What if they're both at home but neither one speaks English
And students, we teach lessons like:
Always treat others the way you want to be treated
But we feed you boring lessons and expect you to be quietly seated
And lock you in detention if your work's not completed
You're the exception that takes the relevance to our rule and deletes it
But we still say you should keep it
Students
We give assignments that seem like they don't matter
But don't blame us, we're just a step on the ladder
Those above us pass down the state standards
They say a multiple-choice test
Is the single-most-important measure of success
And they give the most money to the schools that do best
But give less
To the schools who score poorly because they are poor
But that makes sense, to the schools that do best, give more

Like, maybe the poor schools will fix themselves if they are ignored

Even if their solutions are ones they can't afford

I hope this message gets to the Educational Board

Students, I'm sorry

This world has amazing things out there to discover

But we'd rather give you a classical novel and force you to read cover to cover

And if for some reason, you can't sit through our mind-numbing lesson

It's our suggestion

That you be labeled

As disabled

And we teach you to infer

But we don't think practically

Like we can't concur

That actually

You don't learn well in a system designed to prepare you to work in a factory

We tell you to make claims with evidence

But we don't analyze ourselves factually

Like last year there were over a million dropouts

And we blame them, but that's just a copout

Cuz we don't want to admit that maybe it's partially our fault

And this brings me to my main subject

Forcing you to sit through school is a crime, and we are the main suspects

But if the system is that bad and you really hate it

Wouldn't you really want to change it

Do you really think dropping out is gonna rearrange it?

See the world doesn't care if you wanna be a gangster

They'll lock you in a cage like they're doing society a favor

Ridding the streets of the danger

And you're not gonna be a changer

locked up as a stranger

I mean if you really want to be a rebel

Be successful

Cuz I know you can

But you need to know you can

And you need to show you can

Dear school kids,

If you really think it's cool

To break the rules

Then do well in school

Oh and by the way, I do follow a teacher

And he broke rules

He was also a preacher

But I can't say his name in schools

But he did tell me something about education

He told me that more information

Won't bring me salvation

He said I could go to college

But all the knowledge

In the world won't bring peace to my psyche

He told me politely

That if I wanted that I had to live rightly

He said, "the only way is to be like me"

So I follow him and I'm free, running like Nike

And I love you but I don't care if you like me

And since I love you, I'm here to tell you the truth

Our system is flawed and there's plenty of proof

So you could quit it

And be another statistic

But if you really want to beat it

Complete it

Cuz our hope for the future, our hope to change the world, is you

So work hard, chase your dreams, and watch them come true

"Dear School Kids," a spoken word poem by TEN20

CAN I STEAL THE BALL FROM THE QUARTERBACK?

One thing I regret in life is not playing every year of youth football. I didn't play football from 4th–7th grade and, boy, did I miss out. The reason I didn't play for those years is because my football experience was tainted by my first season in third grade. Due to my family's annual cabin trip, I missed the first two weeks of practices. In addition, I had never really watched football and didn't understand the game or how it worked.

When I finally made it to practice, all the good positions were taken. They stuck me at defensive end. Not glamorous at all. I hadn't watched much football, but I at least knew about quarterbacks, running backs, and wide receivers. I had big dreams of scoring touchdowns and spiking the ball in the endzone. Nope. Defensive end. Eventually, the coaches realized I was actually fast and athletic. They tried me at some other positions, but my lack of understanding of the game led to underwhelming results. At the end of a disappointing season—my team was one of the worst in the league—I decided to stick with baseball and hockey.

When we press into God, we start to have ideas of the big and amazing things that He could do in and through our lives. Sometimes, when we share these ideas with others, they are met with doubts. Excuses. Reasons it could never work.

Despite the result of the season as a whole, there were some highlights, such as a kick-return touchdown—I may be the only player ever to play D-end and kick returner. But best of all was the highlight that no one saw coming. I had never seen such a play in my life, and I have yet to see anything like it.

It all started with the car ride to a game one Saturday morning. I was starting to get the feel for playing D-end. It was sort of boring, though. I felt like I could add more to the game.

"Dad?" I inquired.

"Yeah?"

"Can I steal the ball from the quarterback?"

He paused, pondering the question.

"Ummm, sure, I guess."

On the first play of the game, I lined up across from the offensive tackle and smiled to myself. I had the perfect plan. As the ball was hiked, I stepped right, head-faking with conviction. As the boy across from me stepped with me, I knew my plan was about to work. With a swim move back to the left, I was through the line and into the backfield. The quarterback held the ball out for his teammate. To his utter confusion, I snatched the ball out of his hands, put a Madden '07 truck stick on the running back, and was off to the races in the opposite direction. I don't remember scoring, so I'm pretty sure the quarterback tracked me down. What I do remember is that everyone was amazed. My dad recalls returning from his coffee run after missing the best play of my athletic career, and the other parents recounting the story to him with enthusiasm.

Having not seen much football, I didn't understand what the big deal was. I thought I had just made a regular play and didn't understand why people didn't do that more often.

Now, I think of life in terms of this play. I'm thankful for my dad and how he answered my question that day. He could have said, "I've never seen that before. That's impossible. That's unlikely. I doubt you can do it." Instead, he said yes.

When we press into God, we start to have ideas of the big and amazing things that He could do in and through our lives. Sometimes, when we share these ideas with others, they are met with doubts. Excuses. Reasons it could never work. I have come to realize that people who respond in such a way aren't ill-intentioned. They aren't "haters." They are actually trying to help. They don't want you to set your hopes too high and then be disappointed and hurt.

People are just doing for you what they have done in their own lives. Doubt. Make excuses. Succumb to fear. Scared to think outside the box. Afraid to take risks. They don't want to be hurt or disappointed. Most people never pursue the things that God puts in their hearts because they are too afraid. They have been told their idea is impossible.

You know what is impossible? Feeding five thousand men and their families with two fish and five loaves of bread. Ask your Father what He wants to do in your life. Ask Him what is possible. We don't have to have fish and bread for thousands of people. We just need to bring Him what we have and let Him do the rest.

"If you can'?" said Jesus. "Everything is possible for one who believes" (Mark 9:23).

THE MILLION-DOLLAR QUESTION

What do you want to be when you grow up? The million-dollar question. The question we've been asked ever since we were little. We're expected to have a good answer by the time we're 18, so we can pick a major in college.

Well, I was now turning 22 soon and still didn't have the answer. The opening poem to this chapter was written during my time as a student teacher. The deeper I got into the education system, the more I realized how it was failing our youth, and the less I wanted to be a part of it. It's not to say there aren't many great educators and administrators out there who are doing their very best to create change and empower young people. There are. I applaud them and encourage anyone with such passion to go into the field. I simply began to realize more and more that it wasn't for me. I was at a crossroads. I was approaching graduation and was engaged to Abigail. Our wedding was scheduled for June 25th, and she still had a semester of school to finish the next Fall. We were soon going to launch our young family and be completely dependent on my income. The problem was I didn't want to be a teacher.

If I didn't want to teach, what did I want to do? That was the problem. I didn't know. Earlier that year, I had been praying about what my next steps in life were. I had a sort of vision in my mind that I felt strongly had been given by God. The only way I can describe the vision is that I saw myself doing a relational youth ministry in the inner-city. I prayed and said to God that I would follow wherever He was leading me; it was just up to Him to open and close the right doors. I also knew that I was meant to keep performing spoken word poetry and that I loved Christian hip-hop.

There were two main problems. I couldn't make any money doing spoken word poetry. I didn't have any social media and, therefore, didn't have a single follower. I didn't know anyone within the Christian hip-hop world, didn't have a microphone, and had no idea how to take my art to the next level. I also found no open full-time jobs in youth ministry in the Twin Cities. I did Google searches every day and couldn't find anything. I knew I wanted to pursue ministry and poetry, but it just seemed impossible.

A Fortunate Accident

Since Bethel University is a liberal arts school, there are certain categories of liberal arts courses that every student has to take. One of these categories is an "A-course" that focuses on one of many art forms. You can choose an instrument, drawing, painting, ceramics, jazz dance, and more. I had taken piano lessons from 3rd–6th grade, so I chose to take Beginning Piano. I figured I could slip by with an easy A and maintain my 4.0 GPA.

When I was younger, I despised my piano lessons, partially because I thought it was uncool to play piano and partially because there was no good reason for me to want to play "Hot Cross Buns." Anyone who's taken piano lessons knows what I'm talking about! I even recorded myself pounding on the keys, using a tape recorder, and then played it from the basement, so my mom would think I was practicing while I was really winning the Superbowl on Madden on my Xbox.

> I couldn't make any money doing spoken word poetry. I didn't have any social media and, therefore, didn't have a single follower. I didn't know anyone within the Christian hip-hop world, didn't have a microphone, and had no idea how to take my art to the next level.

The second time around, however, I began to fall in love with the piano. I would go up to the practice rooms and teach myself songs or make up chord progressions. Despite how much I practiced, I barely earned an A in the class since I wouldn't actually practice the class material. One day, I was playing a chord progression and started reciting a poem while I played. Before I knew it, I was rapping. Yes, the first time I rapped was by accident.

From that point on, though, I began writing several songs and recording them on my phone as I played the piano. The recordings sounded horrible, but I could tell that when it came to my lyrics and vocals, the potential was there. I started to ponder how awesome it would be to be a rapper. I thought about how much music had impacted me and how I could do the same thing for someone else. When it came down to it, however, I talked myself out of it. I felt I had no business being a rapper, and I didn't show my songs to anyone.

Güero Rapero

Have you ever noticed that certain people won't cuss in their native language but as soon as they learn a bad word in another language, they start using it regularly? There is something about using another language that can take away one's inhibitions. That Spring, I had the opportunity to return to Guatemala for a week. I would be working with Marcos, playing sports, and sharing the love of Jesus with kids in several communities. I was still scared to rap for people in English, but for some reason, I thought it would be cool to write a rap in Spanish that I could perform for the kids. Before I got on the plane, I downloaded an instrumental onto my phone. During the plane ride, I wrote an entire rap song in Spanish. On the first day, I performed my song for Marcos to see what he thought. From that moment, Marcos became my first promoter. Everywhere we went, he told everyone that I was a *güero rapero*, which means white rapper, and had me rap my song.

Everywhere.

Not just with the kids we played sports with—Marcos would have me rap for friends he walked by on the street. Everyone seemed to love my song. Sometimes, we would play with the same kids a few days later, and they would start rapping my song when they saw me. Though my "success" rapping in Guatemala didn't seem like a big deal—and was somewhat exhausting—it was a huge step for me to get over my fears and insecurities. There is a quote that says, "You don't have to be great to get started, but you do have to get started to become great." To anyone with a dream, you don't have to have it all figured out, but I hope I can encourage you to take a step forward.

Coincidence...?

Have you ever felt like God was trying to tell you something? In one week, there were multiple situations that happened when I felt God was calling me to make music. The week culminated with attending an Andy Mineo concert on his "Uncomfortable" tour that featured Propaganda—two of my favorite artists. As I rapped every word to their songs, I began to realize I could see myself up on stage. The next day, I woke up early and couldn't go back to sleep. I decided to get to work. I went to the Apple App Store and downloaded Garageband onto my iPhone 6. Over the next few hours, I taught myself how to use Garageband, made a beat, wrote a song to my beat, and recorded it through the mic on my Apple headphones.

The song was called "Utopia" and was meant to expose the emptiness of pursuing the "American Dream" without knowing God and His purpose for our lives. The following week, I brought the song to Dr. Claudia May, a professor of reconciliation studies at Bethel University, who loves Christian hip-hop. To my surprise, she loved my song. She even asked me to perform it at her upcoming hip-hop event that she was hosting. I performed through my nerves and told the audience that I had produced the song on my iPhone and was looking for an actual producer. Sure enough, the keynote speaker that night, Benny Roberts, approached me at the end of the event. He told me that he loved my song. He said he had about 1,000 original beats on his laptop and a home studio where I could record, free of charge. Just like that, my music career was born.

PERFECT TIMING

Benny is a casual, independent producer who didn't exactly have a million-dollar record deal to offer me, so I still had to figure out how I was going to make money. I hadn't had any luck Google searching ministry jobs, so I figured I would apply to some teaching jobs just in case. I had a good interview at a school not far from where we wanted to live and was fairly confident they would offer me the job. The job was for an ESL teacher at an elementary school. Not only did I not want to teach, but I especially didn't want to teach elementary school.

But even greater than my desire not to teach elementary school was my desire not to be unemployed. I applied to several high school jobs but kept getting denied. I figured that as a bilingual male with a 4.0 GPA and a vast amount of extracurricular experience, it would be easy to find a job. This was not the case. I started to wonder whether my vision for inner-city ministry had actually been from God or had it just been wishful thinking. I definitely didn't want to teach elementary school, but it was starting to look like the only option.

My wedding was rapidly approaching, which meant I needed to figure out where my paycheck would be coming from. Amidst the endless amount of Google searches and job applications, I got an email out of the blue that turned the tide. The email was from Carrie Kotke, who had been the Area Director for Young Life when I was a leader there. I had told her that I wanted to do urban ministry, but I hadn't heard anything from her in months. Attached to the email was a job description that seemed too good to be true. The job was a new Young Life start up program at a high school in Minneapolis. It was as if I had written the job description myself with what I wanted, and it had now been sent to me in an email. I applied immediately and was chosen to enter into the interview process.

It came down to a week before our wedding. We didn't know where I was going to work or where we were going to live. I had a meeting scheduled with the elementary school offering the ESL teaching position for Friday at noon. I was fairly sure they were going to offer me the job, which I really didn't want, and would ask me to make a decision as soon as possible. In my Young Life interviews, I was told I could hear back from them as early as that same Friday. All morning I hoped and prayed I would hear back from Young Life; I couldn't stop refreshing my inbox to see if I got an email. Nothing.

It was 11:30 a.m. and I was walking out to my car to head to the elementary school meeting. I decided to look at my phone one more time before I typed the school address into Google Maps. There it was! The email I had been waiting for—the job offer from Young Life! I called the school immediately and told them I wasn't coming in. Abigail and I hopped in the car, drove down to south Minneapolis, and signed a lease for our first apartment. Everything was set. We were getting married, had our own place, had the perfect job, and I was even launching my music career.

Little did I know, I was heading into a trial that would change my life forever.

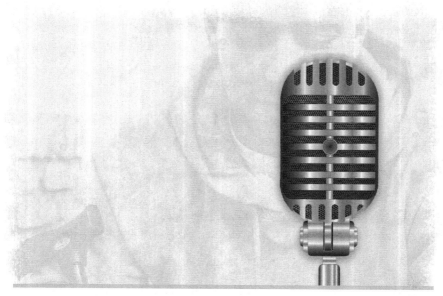

CHAPTER 12

THE CALM BEFORE THE STORM

So we cared for you. Because we loved you so much, we were delighted to share with you not only the gospel of God but our lives as well.

— 1 Thessalonians 2:8

I'm in a rundown, time chasing after me
I'm living happily
But trials come, and that's the way it has to be
Ain't living passively
I'm changed drastically
And I ain't scared, I know Who's looking after me
No more fear, yeah I'm all in
Making moves and I hear the Lord calling

I'ma answer now, no more stalling
No excuses, He'll catch me if I'm falling

An excerpt from "No Excuses," a song by TEN20

https://www.youtube.com/watch?v=6QEwJR7E3q0

FULL CIRCLE

My life took a very fast transition. The day Abigail and I got back from our honeymoon, we moved into our apartment, and I started my new job. It was July 5, 2016. I went from living in the suburbs my entire life and being financially dependent on my parents, to living in south Minneapolis and having to balance a budget and pay the bills. After my Young Life orientation, I sat down in my office with the daunting yet exciting task in front of me: to start a new program.

I had zero connections on the southside and literally didn't know anyone from the community. To make matters more interesting, my supervisor was off serving at camp, so I didn't have any training or direction. Luckily, my supervisor was friends with the wife of the head football coach at the high school I was supposed to work with. She sent me the coach's number, and the first thing I did as a new employee was give him a call. Sure enough, he answered. After I told him I had coached high school football for two years and was running a teen mentoring program in the community, I was hired on the spot.

As the school year started, I headed to the school one day to see if I could volunteer. I figured it would be an easy sell. I had an education license, was bilingual, was a football coach, and ran a mentoring program in the community. I just wanted to help, and from what I could tell, the school needed all the help it could get. I thought they'd be thrilled to have me there. Well, I was wrong. I was not received warmly by the reception desk. I explained who I was, my credentials, and that I wanted to volunteer. The receptionist looked at me and said, "Well, thanks, but I think we're all good."

That could have been the end of the story, but I would not go away that easily. My area director and boss had given me the name of one school administrator who was a believer and was on board with Young Life. I had never met her, but I felt she was my best bet. I stated the administrator's name and asked if I could speak with her. I was directed to her office. That was all I needed. Before long, I was volunteering in multiple classrooms every week and was helping to supervise lunch in addition to coaching football.

As I continued building relationships with the teens, I started to invite them to Young Life. They were very skeptical at first, but who can say no to a hot meal, games, and a ride home, instead of walking or taking the city bus, which were the most common alternatives. I felt like part of why God had called me to Minneapolis was to be a bridge-builder, specifically for people of different ethnicities. When Fall camp came around, my cabin of leaders and teens included young men who were White, Black, Native American, Latino, Somali, and Hmong. It was truly beautiful.

> When you make yourself available to God, He can do more than you could ever ask or imagine.

As time went on, the ministry continued to grow. We had our weekly club gatherings; frequent dinners and Bible studies in my home; church-league basketball, which eventually grew into a traveling AAU team; amazing camp trips; and true friendships. I can only marvel at how God brings things full-circle. My Young Life leaders had a profound impact on me and coached me in football, baseball, and church-league basketball. While in college, I had led Young Life and coached my group of teens in the same three sports. Now I was getting to do the same thing as a job. Over time, the school even warmed up to me—they eventually even offered me a classroom and a key to the school! Based on my first encounter with the front desk, I never would have thought this possible. But, when you make yourself available to God, He can do more than you could ever ask or imagine.

HOLE 6

I have never been a great golfer. I've never understood how I could hit a fast-moving baseball so well but couldn't hit a stationary golf ball to save my life. My family members, besides my brother Rick, weren't much better.

Regardless of how bad we were, my family still made sure we went golfing a few times each year. There is a pretty cheap course just miles away from our cabin, Oakwood. Oakwood is cheap due to its poor conditions, which has earned it the nickname, "Jokewood." One day many years before, my parents and I went out to play nine holes. My parents decided to splurge and get a cart. *Yes! I can't wait to drive!* To my disappointment, they didn't let me drive for the first few holes because I was too young, and we were still in view of the clubhouse. After what felt like an eternity—partially due to not being able to drive the cart, and partially due to not being able to drive the ball—we got to hole 6.

We were out of view of the clubhouse, and it was my time to shine. I was ready to go. I had waited six holes too long and was eager to put the pedal to the metal. My parents and I hopped into the cart.

"Take it easy," my dad cautioned. *Yeah, right.* I floored it. I quickly realized that although I thought the wheel was pointed straight, it was actually turned one full rotation to the right. To the right of the tee box was a ball washer, a bench, and a garbage can. I was headed straight for them. No problem. I slammed my foot down on the break—so I thought. Instead, my foot slammed down yet again on the gas pedal, propelling the golf cart toward the course accessories. The ball washer went down like a quarterback sacked blindsided by a defensive lineman (before all these new rules protecting quarterbacks). The bench and the garbage can followed suit. To this day, my family laughs about this story, and the dented garbage can remains on hole 6.

I released a 5-track EP called *No Excuses* on June 16, 2016. I figured that within a few months, I would be on tour and have a record deal... Nope.

A ROUGH START

While my job was going great, I didn't know which direction my music career was headed. As the golf cart story illustrates, I was eager to start, determined to put the pedal to the medal. In college, I had put out a spoken word poetry video called *The Cure*. I had no social media at the time, so I created an account on YouTube and uploaded the video. I asked Abigail to share it on Facebook. The video got 2,000 views overnight, along with an overwhelming amount of positive feedback. I figured my music would take off in the same way, but to an even greater extent. I released a 5-track EP called *No Excuses* on June 16, 2016. I figured that within a few months, I would be on tour and have a record deal... Nope.

My EP did get a good response overall, but no major record labels or music venues were calling me. I went against my gut instincts and got into a sort of backhanded deal with a more established rapper. He promised to book me paid shows each month. It sounded like a perfect opportunity to grow my music career! I could do a paid show every month, sell merchandise, grow my fanbase, and most of all, inspire people and help them to know God. The only caveat was I had to buy into his pyramid scheme business. My judgment was clouded by my desire to grow my music career, so I agreed.

Months went by... Not one show was booked and not one dollar was made. I felt cheated, tricked, ashamed, and angry. Needless to say, I left the pyramid scheme. I want to say I have since reconciled with this individual. He is a great man, artist, and minister. We had a lot of miscommunication and misunderstanding, and I was not yet very mature. Soon after, I got a call from an "agent" who said he could get me a $300,000 deal with Warner Bros. Records. After searching this "agent" on Google, I found out this too was a scam. My introduction to the music industry was certainly not pleasant, but I was determined not to give up.

I then got connected with a small Christian record label that agreed to work with me, but I still had to pay out of pocket to produce my music. I nearly emptied our savings account to produce my next EP with the idea that I would make money now that I was working with a label... Wrong again. Working with this label was an experience I will forever cherish, though. I learned so much about making high-quality music. My first video hit around 50,000 views, and I had my first few successful shows. However, I still didn't see a single penny. I started to learn that the music industry wasn't as simple as I had previously and naively thought.

SCAN OR VISIT

https://album.link/us/i/1183111644

The Calm

As I started to grow in my identity as an artist, I started to realize that the label and I were headed in different directions, so I decided to move on. I released a mixtape and another EP on my own and began to slowly grow my brand. I had several successful shows, started selling CDs and t-shirts, and even made some money. I got to open up for one of my all-time favorite artists, Dee-1. I also opened for Datin, an artist from God Over Money, one of my favorite record labels.

https://album.link/us/i/1315675988

Work was great, music was good, marriage was wonderful, but everything was about to change.

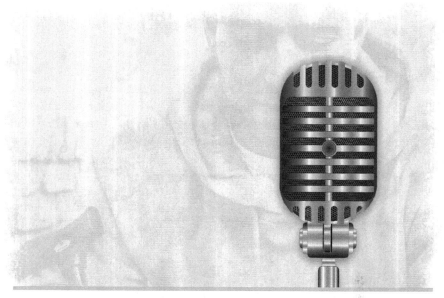

CHAPTER 13

TIME TO FACE THE MUSIC

Then the man said, "Your name will no longer be Jacob, but Israel, because you have struggled with God and with humans and have overcome."

— Genesis 32:28

Cuz I don't see You
And I don't hear You
Trying to believe You
Tryna fear You
I wonder if You hear me
If You're there, could You please come near me?

An excerpt from "Hard Days," a song by TEN20

JACOB

I sometimes wonder how much significance our names have in determining the direction of our lives. In the Bible, Jacob wrestled with God until he received a blessing. In the process, he suffered a dislocated hip. It wasn't easy, but he refused to give up. He endured physical pain but refused to surrender. He demanded an answer. Some people think that God is not to be questioned. They point to Bible verses like Isaiah 45:9–10 and say the clay must not question the potter.

I believe that God can handle our questions. I would even say that God invites our laments. Throughout the Scriptures, there are examples of godly men and women who cried out to God in agony—the prophets, king David, and even Jesus. When Israel cried out to God from Egypt, He heard their cries and brought deliverance. Jacob wrestled with God until God blessed him and thus became the father of God's people, Israel. It may be coincidence that my parents named me Jacob, but God and I were headed into our fiercest wrestling match yet.

EVEN MORE RUSTINESS?

I wrote earlier about the first few times I started to wonder about my physical health. The time I fell down while making a cut in flag football. When I trained with AIT in South Carolina and was shaky while lifting weights.

> I figured maybe I was rusty, but even after a few times on the ice, my skills didn't come back. In my mind, I still knew how to skate, but I couldn't translate the movements from my mind to my body.

Well, similar experiences continued to occur as time went on. During college I went out to skate with Abigail, who happened to play hockey in college as well as softball. When I got out on the ice, I had trouble skating well. I could maintain balance but couldn't sprint or make sharp turns. When I was younger, skating was like walking. I learned when I was 3 years old, and it was second nature. I figured maybe I was rusty, but even after a few times on the ice, my skills didn't come back. In my mind, I still knew how to skate, but I couldn't translate the movements from my mind to my body. I would even have dreams in which I remembered how to skate again, but then I'd wake up and the memory would fade. It was so depressing that I gave up skating altogether.

Abigail also had bought me a pair of roller blades. Again, I learned to blade at a young age, so it used to be easy for me, but when I put my new roller blades on, I couldn't even maintain my balance. I couldn't figure out what was happening. They say if you don't use it, you lose it. That was the only explanation I could think of. I was still more physically fit than most people and could beat several of my friends, who were college football players, in racquetball. The thought that I had something seriously wrong in my body never crossed my mind.

FIRST IMPRESSIONS

Have you ever talked with your good friends about your first impression of each other? It can be a humbling experience in two ways. One, we realize how bad of a first impression we can give! Two, we realize how quick we are to judge others and how wrong we were about the people who are now our good friends. I started to notice a recurring theme in my friends' first impressions of me. "I thought you were drunk." "I thought you were high." "I thought you were a stoner." "I thought you were a big partier." I would get this again and again. It always ended with something like, "But now I know you're just a chill person."

When I first started hearing that everyone thought I abused substances, I was troubled. I remember sitting down to a meal with Abigail and expressing my concern. Why does everyone think this? How can I represent Jesus when everyone thinks I'm high on drugs? She explained that how I talk resembles someone who is drunk or high. But I had never smoked or drank in my life and had mostly avoided the party scene, so my frame of reference for how people act under the influence was limited.

Abigail encouraged me to embrace who I was, and that's what I did. She promised that anyone who took the time to get to know me would see who I really was; if someone didn't take that time, then who cares what they think anyway? I became comfortable with how I talk and determined that being "chill" was just part of my personality.

THE SILVER BULLET

From 2014–2018, I drove the '02 Jeep Grand Cherokee that I had inherited from my dad. I called it the Silver Bullet. When I first started driving it, I noticed that the engine made a ticking noise. I don't know much about cars, but I know that a tick in the engine is not supposed to happen. I quickly got a cassette tape-to-auxiliary cord, played my music in the car, and forgot all about the engine tick. If you've ever had a tape-to-aux cord—this is what you used before Bluetooth—you know they don't last long. After a few months, the cord would fray and stop working. At that point, I would order a new cord on Amazon. I couldn't really stand the music on the radio, so I'd usually ride in silence.

Tick, tick, tick... I would notice the tick while I waited for my aux cord to come in the mail. Then, I would get my new cord, turn the music back on, and forget the tick again. Now and then, someone would ride in my car for the first time. Sometimes, they would ask me about the tick. "Oh, yeah. It ticks, but it still works fine."

This '02 Jeep Grand Cherokee well illustrates what was happening with my body. Most of the time, I didn't notice anything wrong. Every once in a while, though, I would notice the proverbial tick. Like when I tried wakeboarding and could no longer land jumps. Or when I tried slalom water skiing and could no longer get up on one ski. Or when I played softball and couldn't track a pop-fly. In those moments, I would stop and wonder if something was wrong.

> Every once in a while, though, I would notice the proverbial tick. Like when I tried wakeboarding and could no longer land jumps. Or when I tried slalom water skiing and could no longer get up on one ski. Or when I played softball and couldn't track a pop-fly. In those moments, I would stop and wonder if something was wrong.

But before I knew it, I was back on the racquetball or basketball court, or simply going about my daily life, and everything was just fine. People who met me for the first time noticed the "tick." I talked funny and walked funny. As they got to know me, though, they too would say, "Sure, it ticks, but it still works fine." I started to subconsciously avoid situations where my "ticks" might come out. I was busy during alumni baseball games. I didn't invite my friends to wakeboard. I didn't do certain workouts that required a high level of balance. I kept turning the music up louder and louder to avoid hearing the ticks.

Eventually, the music couldn't get any louder. I was forced to listen to the ticks. It was time to figure out what was wrong.

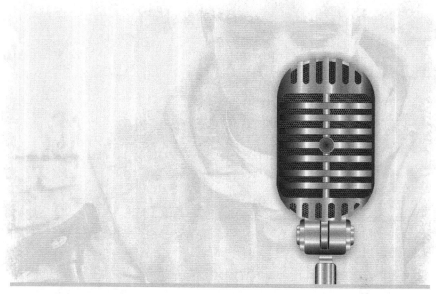

CHAPTER 14

THE STORM

How long, Lord? Will you forget me forever? How long will you hide your face from me? How long must I wrestle with my thoughts and day after day have sorrow in my heart? How long will my enemy triumph over me?

— Psalm 13:1–2

I just wanna go back to when everything was easier
Before the doctor told me that "you have a disease in you
And that's why your body don't work like it used to
You might have trouble walking in the future"
And I remember running faster than all of my peers
But now I'm having trouble going up and down the stairs
I'm only 24 and I'm tryna be hopeful
Some days it feels I'm at the end of my rope though

An excerpt from "Hard Days," a song by TEN20

111

https://song.link/us/i/1489544406

THE UNSHARPENED PENCIL

I was riding in the backseat of my friend's car one day and noticed that in the pocket of the seat in front of me was an unsharpened pencil. For some reason, this pencil caught my eye, and I couldn't stop thinking about it. Then it hit me. This pencil had so much potential. So many stories that could be written. So many equations that could be solved. This pencil was limitless. There was one problem, though. It hadn't been sharpened. It dawned on me that until this pencil is sharpened, it will never reach its potential and fulfill its purpose!

The sharpening process is painful. There is friction, cutting away, and loss. There is so much potential within each and every one of us. We all have been created with a purpose. For us to get there, though, there will be friction. There will be cutting away. There will be pain. There will be loss.

My appointment with the sharpener had arrived.

https://www.facebook.com/1081594375262750/videos/379134956771096

THE COOL COUSIN

Everybody has that "cool cousin." Joe was my cool cousin. He was muscular, had tattoos, wore stylish clothes, dated cute girls, and was in a band. As a pre-teen boy, I aspired to be just like Joe. One year, when I was 11 or 12, both our immediate families went to Florida together for Spring Break. Joe was a boarder—snowboard, skateboard, wakeboard, anything you could stand on and ride. When he and I saw people skimboarding, we knew we had to try it. If you don't know, in skimboarding, you hold a thin board (like a wider skate-board with no wheels), start running, set the board down (ideally in shallow water), jump on it, and ride it as far as you can. We convinced our parents to buy us skimboards. We were both naturals and spent the majority of the rest of the week honing our skills.

THE STRAW THAT BROKE THE CAMEL'S BACK

On the spectrum of physical activities, skimboarding is on the more difficult end. It takes real speed to get going, coordination to drop and land on the board, and balance to stay up. I spent a lot of time in my younger years doing every type of water sport. Skimboarding, slalom skiing, kneeboarding, wakeboarding, wakeskating, and wakesurfing. All of these (other than kneeboarding) are watersports that take a good amount of skill and athleti-cism, and I could do them well. Then there is paddle boarding, which is simply stand-ing on a surfboard with a two-ended paddle and paddling. It is a way to enjoy nature—the watersport equivalent to hiking.

> The "ticks" could no longer be ignored—they were now louder than the music. As I fell off the paddleboard time and time again, my illusion that everything was okay finally came crashing down along with me into the water.

I was now 24 years old and was back in Florida with my family for Spring Break. At Abigail's request, we rented a paddleboard for an hour. Abigail went out first and paddled around with ease, so I decided to give it a try. What happened next was a turning point in my life.

No, I did not get attacked by a shark. I tried again and again, but couldn't maintain my balance to stay standing on the board. How is it that I spent my formative years doing much more difficult activities and now I couldn't even paddleboard? I was supposed to be in my athletic prime. The "ticks" could no longer be ignored—they were now louder than the music. As I fell off the paddleboard time and time again, my illusion that everything was okay finally came crashing down along with me into the water.

Everything wasn't okay.

A SOBERING APPOINTMENT

My experience with the paddleboard forced me to ask the question, "Why do I have such bad balance?" Even my dad, who is an ER doctor, couldn't give me an answer. As I considered my symptoms and thought about my past experiences, I came up with one potential solution. I had recently been hit in the head with a basketball, decently hard. Since then, I had been experiencing some dizziness and sensitivity to light. I knew from my training as a football coach that these were concussion symptoms.

Then, I thought about all the hits to the head I had taken throughout my life. The time I got checked from behind in a hockey game, sending me headfirst into the boards and then playing the rest of the game with double vision. The time I got popped in a football game, and my chin went numb for a week. The many other hits I had taken to the head playing football and hockey. I never once went to the doctor or sat out. I started to wonder if several undiagnosed concussions had impacted my balance. I told my theory to my dad, and we decided I should see a physical therapist that specialized in balance.

My first physical therapy appointment was sobering. Over the last few years, I had avoided pretty much anything that exposed my bad balance. At PT, I was forced to do exercises specifically designed to do just that. It was apparent right away that something wasn't right. I was lacking in balance and coordination, and was testing far below where I should have for age 24.

The physical therapist gave me several workouts to do at home, and I began doing them diligently, devoting 30 minutes to an hour daily just on my PT, in addition to my regular workouts. I was determined to regain the physical abilities I had lost. I wanted to get back on a wakeboard, on my skates, on the court.

After about a month of physical therapy, I was showing a lot of improvement but was still nowhere near "normal." My physical therapist was convinced there was a deeper issue beyond my concussion hypothesis, so I was referred to a neurologist.

ATAXIA

I hadn't seen a doctor in eight years. Now, here I was, seeing a neurologist and getting an MRI on my brain. The neurologist asked me several questions about my symptoms, and then I underwent the MRI. In addition, I gave eight different blood samples to test for any irregularities. I was set to have a follow up appointment to get my MRI and blood test results.

The neurologist said the one word that would forever change my life: Ataxia. He said I had Ataxia, which is basically a blanket term for a loss of control of bodily movements. Ataxia can have many different causes. Vitamin deficiencies, genetic mutations, brain damage, and alcoholism, to name a few. When you search Ataxia on Google, you'll find things like *difficulty walking, talking, swallowing, tremors, loss of vision.* I thought my doctor must be mistaken. I could walk, talk, see, and swallow just fine. There was no way I had Ataxia.

BOB ALLISON

On my way out, a woman at the reception desk gave me a pamphlet about Ataxia. One part of that pamphlet instantly caught my eye. It was the story of a former pro baseball player, Bob Allison. A few years after retiring, Bob returned to play in an alumni game. He was flat-out embarrassed. He couldn't track fly balls, throw accurately, or even run the bases well.

I was immediately reminded of a similar situation I had endured in college. Sure, I was never a pro, but I had been a solid baseball player growing up. One time in college, I went out to play softball with some friends. I was in the outfield, and a routine pop-up was hit in my direction. I tried tracking it down, but for some reason, I couldn't. The ball landed on the ground a few feet from me. I was so embarrassed.

The Allison story in this pamphlet caused several similar memories to surface. The time I went out for a football pass, and instead of me catching it, it hit me in the shoulder. The time I took ground balls with Abigail's family and couldn't make an accurate throw to first base. I could relate to this story, and it made me wonder if I actually did have Ataxia. I had so many unanswered questions and unexplained situations regarding my health. Maybe Ataxia was the answer and the explanation that I was looking for.

CONNECTING THE DOTS

When I got home, I told Abigail what my doctor had said. I was still not convinced he was right. Married folks, however, know that sometimes our spouses are the best ones at humbling us! I protested that I didn't have difficulty walking or talking. She reminded me that I often got off balance walking from the bed to the bathroom. I argued that the floor was slanted—which was true as the house was 100 years old—and that I was usually tired when this happened. She replied that although both of those facts were true, she never lost her balance like I did.

She also reminded me that people often think I am drunk or high because of my slurred speech. I had come to accept this as part of my personality, but she pointed out that it was also a symptom of Ataxia. She also graciously reminded me of several times when I tripped and was unable to regain my balance. Although she had made some good points, I could still walk and talk fine, and doubted that I actually had Ataxia.

Having a dad who is an ER doctor comes with its perks— someone to stitch you up at home, prescribe you the right medicine, or just tell you to rub some dirt in it. Also, I never had to wait for my follow up appointments to get my test results because my dad had access to them, with my full permission, of course, as soon as they were uploaded.

I thought another possibility was that I had suffered brain damage from various concussions, and an even worse possibility that I had a brain tumor. My dad looked at my MRI images and determined they were completely normal. His only concern was that my brain was too small (a Dr. joke). He looked at my blood test results and confirmed that all my levels were normal as well. This news was good and bad. The good news was I didn't have brain damage or a tumor. From what we could tell, I wasn't dying. The bad news was we still didn't know what was wrong.

My follow up appointment was with an Ataxia specialist. The medical team explained that whether or not I had Ataxia was the wrong question; given my symptoms, it was obvious. The question at hand was *why* I had Ataxia. They had ruled out several possibilities with my MRI and blood tests. The doctor explained that since my Ataxia had nothing to do with brain damage or blood levels, the cause was likely either genetic or something impossible to diagnose.

His hypothesis was I had Friedreich's Ataxia. This is a recessive, genetic disorder that causes progressive damage to the cerebral cortex, leading to Ataxia.

This rare disease affects 1 in 50,000 people. If the doctor was right, it meant I had lived with Friedreich's Ataxia (FA) my entire life. Both my parents would have unknowingly carried FA recessively, and together passed it on to me. This would explain why my symptoms were less dramatic. It would also mean my symptoms would only get worse. People with Friedreich's Ataxia will likely end up wheelchair-bound and die early from heart complications. I gave more blood for genetic testing. This test would confirm whether or not I had FA. This test would change my life forever.

I had about a month to process what the doctor had said while I awaited my test results. I thought back on my entire life. I had come to terms with the fact that God must not have made me to be a professional athlete. I had chalked up the athletic success of my younger years to being an early bloomer.

But then, I started to think about my life through the lens of FA. When I was a boy, I was stronger and faster than almost all of my peers. I had a strong, accurate throwing arm, good hands, and quick feet. I could do difficult things like skimboarding and slalom water skiing. Through my teen years, I maintained my strength and speed, which allowed me to be successful in sports; however, there were certain things that I did in an unorthodox manner.

The medical team explained that whether or not I had Ataxia was the wrong question; given my symptoms, it was obvious. The question at hand was *why* I had Ataxia.

On my state championship baseball team of 15-year-olds, I hit third in the batting order—that's where one of the best hitters goes—and led my team in stolen bases. I once stole six bases in one game! Despite my speed, though, my coach still joked that I ran funny. I also wasn't the best in the field when it came to defense. They stuck me in right field, and I could hold my own, but my offensive skills were what kept me in the starting lineup.

Through the lens of FA, it started to make sense. Fielding takes a lot of balance and coordination. You have to be able to sprint while looking up at the ball and remain steady enough to make the catch. Then, you have to properly coordinate your crow-hop—a footwork technique for long throws—and arm motion to make a strong, accurate throw. Batting is more about having good timing, reading the pitcher, and having a mechanically sound swing; when you bat, you are standing still, which takes out the challenge of remaining steady and balanced. I was always a good hitter, but as the years went on, my fielding never improved—it actually got worse. This is one of countless examples that began to make sense as I looked at my life through the FA perspective. *Do I really have FA?*

After what felt like an eternity, the results came back.

The answer was yes.

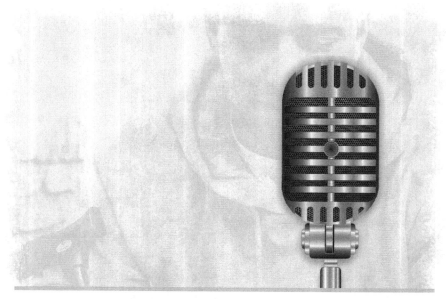

CHAPTER 15

A FIRM FOUNDATION

Why did I ever come out of the womb to see trouble and sorrow and to end my days in shame?
— Jeremiah 20:18

The storm rages
I'm looking at a Bible full of torn pages
Like do you really care for me?
And are you really there for me?
I've had a lot of people tell me that they're gonna say a prayer for me
But nothing changes so I got questions
They say in the hard times we get taught lessons
But I'm sick of hearing those cliches
Man I've heard it all before

And I need something more

These days

Like can't you see that I'm hurting?

And truth is that me and depression been flirting

And hopelessness calls every night and every morning

I don't know how long I can keep ignoring

The rain is pouring

They say wait for the rainbow

Like I'm some kind of angel

But I don't have a halo

I lay awake in a bed full of sorrow

Wondering if I have strength just to make it to tomorrow

I know my time is borrowed

But sometimes I wish it would run out

It's so cloudy I can't even see the sun out

I'm just praying for healing

Wondering if you hear me, or if my prayers just hit the ceiling

"Metamorphosis: Part 1," a spoken word poem by TEN20

METAMORPHOSIS

Butterflies are amazing creatures. They gracefully float through the air and radiate beautiful colorways and intricate designs from their wings. Every butterfly, though, was once a less impressive caterpillar. A caterpillar actually has everything it needs to become a butterfly on the inside. But, in order for the caterpillar to transform into the magnificent being that it was destined to be, it must undergo *metamorphosis*. During metamorphosis, the caterpillar spends a significant time in a cocoon.

In plain sight, the cocoon process doesn't look like much is happening. In fact, it almost seems like a hopeless situation. The caterpillar is surrounded by darkness. It is trapped. However, it is during metamorphosis that the caterpillar grows its wings. If someone were to open the cocoon too early, the butterfly would be too weak and underdeveloped. It would not survive, let alone fly.

Have you ever felt trapped? Have you ever felt surrounded by darkness? The potential to fly is within you. "Your condition is not your conclusion." This quote has stuck with me through the years. You may feel like you are in a cocoon, but don't give up.

The darkness will fade.
You will escape the trap.
You are undergoing metamorphosis.
You are growing your wings.

FORESHADOWING

Truth be told, I hated my Language Arts classes. We were forced to read classical novels and try to figure out what Shakespeare was trying to say in what seemed like an entirely different language. We had quizzes on the readings to make sure we actually read and didn't just use SparkNotes. These quizzes asked questions about minor story details, which I no longer remember. I do remember one thing from my 9th grade honors Language Arts class, though: foreshadowing.

Foreshadowing is when authors give hints throughout a story about what is going to happen in the future. Usually, the reader doesn't pick up on these hints when they are first reading the story. Once the plot unfolds, however, the reader wonders how they could have missed such obvious clues!

I performed and spoke from stages, always with the same mission: I wanted to give people hope in Jesus. I always thought God gave me these songs and poems for others. In reality, God was foreshadowing my story. He gave me these songs and poems for myself.

I had spent the last six years writing songs and poems meant to inspire people to persevere through their challenges. I performed and spoke from stages, always with the same mission: I wanted to give people hope in Jesus. I always thought God gave me these songs and poems for others.

In reality, God was foreshadowing my story.

He gave me these songs and poems for myself.

https://song.link/us/i/1183111907

TALK IS CHEAP

I love coaching basketball and football. Without fail, an argument always breaks out between two guys about who is better. They go back and forth and talk about how they could beat each other. I always say the same thing: talk is cheap; just play 1-on-1. That will settle it. It's that simple. We can talk and argue and go back and forth all day, but at some point, words must be put to the test.

Now, my words would be put to the test. Now, it was time to believe everything I had written and preached the last six years. It turns out, this is easier said than done. I had written so much about persevering and having hope, but the fact was I hadn't endured anything very difficult in my life. My grandparents all died before I really knew what was happening, so I had never really experienced the death of a loved one. I grew up with both parents and never struggled financially. I never struggled to fit in. I certainly had my ups and downs but had never truly faced tragedy or significantly difficult circumstances. Well, now, I did. Now, I do. After encouraging so many people, it was time to see if I could be encouraged myself.

BRICK BY BRICK

In chapter two, I shared a verse in which Jesus talks about a foundation. He says the one who hears His words and puts them into practice is like the wise man who built his house on the rock. The storm came and beat against the house, but the house stood strong since it had a firm foundation. The one who hears the words of Jesus and does not put them into practice is like the foolish man who built his house on the sand.

When the storm came, the house was destroyed.

Many people build their proverbial houses on the sand. That is why they aren't able to endure the storms of life. This is why people give up on their goals and aspirations, walk out on their families, turn to drugs and alcohol, and even take their own lives. A house built on sand will be destroyed by the storm. A life built on success will be destroyed by failure. A life built on athletics will be destroyed by injury. A life built on a relationship will be destroyed untimely death. A life built on money will be destroyed by economic crisis. A life and identity built on anything of this world can be destroyed by the storms of this world in an instant. However, a life and identity built on something eternal can *never* be destroyed.

I had spent years building my house on the rock. I am not perfect by any means, but I had spent the last six years of my life doing my best to hear the words of Jesus and putting them into practice.

Now, my words would be put to the test. Now, it was time to believe everything I had written and preached the last six years.

People see a great building, but they can't see the foundation that is making it great. People may see me on a stage or in a video, but they can't see the foundation that lies beneath everything I do. They can't see my daily dedication to study God's Word. They can't see my prayer life. They can't see the many times I have refused to compromise my convictions in the face of temptation. They can't see the many times I have stepped out of my comfort zone to follow the leading of God's Spirit in the face of my own fears.

Everyone wants great results, but not everyone wants to do the difficult things that lead to those results.

Xavier Rhodes, an All-Pro NFL cornerback came to speak to my friend's youth group. He said that it's cool to be seen on TV playing football, but he also talked about all the things that people didn't see—the very things that got him to that level. When everyone was going to college parties, he was in the weight room, watching extra games film, or doing schoolwork.

Every time, I chose to follow Christ. To read my Bible instead of watch TV. To go coach and mentor teens instead of play videogames. To start a house church instead of spending Sunday mornings hung over from partying. To wait until marriage to have sex instead of giving in to temptation. Every time, I was laying a brick, building my foundation on the rock.

https://www.instagram.com/p/B6jegvhhOBR/

Broken Dreams...Again

All that Jesus tells us about the house built on the rock is that it didn't fall. I imagine that it took a beating. There may have been some broken windows and some cracks in the siding. Part of the roof may have been torn off. But the house survived. Before my diagnosis, not being able to skate and roller-blade and being embarrassed by my bad balance were just inconveniences. In one sense, my diagnosis brought clarity to my life because it made sense of what had been happening in my body.

In a much larger sense, it brought pain. Everything I did was a reminder of my new reality. When I went to the gym and saw old people working out, all I could think about was the fact that I'll be in a wheelchair at their age—if I am even alive anymore. When I saw dads out walking and playing with their kids, I was reminded that I will be stuck in a wheelchair, unable to play catch or go for a hike with my wife and kids. Before my diagnosis, I had hoped I could regain my balance and coordination through physical therapy. I had hope for my future. Now, I looked at my future and all I could see was pain and suffering.

> Before my diagnosis, not being able to skate and rollerblade and being embarrassed by my bad balance were just inconveniences. In one sense, my diagnosis brought clarity to my life because it made sense of what had been happening in my body. In a much larger sense, it brought pain.

When I was younger, I dreamt I would one day be a professional athlete. Basically, every boy who grows up playing sports has that same dream, so the fact that it didn't work out wasn't that difficult to cope with. As a young adult, though, I dreamt of becoming a professional hip-hop and spoken word artist. I wanted to make it into a full-time career. I wanted to tour the country and the world while accumulating millions of streams on Spotify and Apple Music. I didn't want to become rich and famous; I just wanted to impact people with my songs and poems. This dream had actually seemed possible. It seemed realistic.

Not anymore. How could I be a hip-hop and spoken word artist if I am slowly going to lose my ability to walk and even talk. I felt like giving up on this dream. I would never be the artist that I hoped to be. Even worse, though, I would never be the husband I hoped to be. The father. The grandfather. The coach. The leader. I didn't only want to give up on music. I wanted to give up on life.

I had no hope for the future.
Things would only get worse.
There was no point.
I wanted to quit.

CHAPTER 16

HUNGRY FOR HOPE

but those who hope in the Lord will renew their strength. They will soar on wings like eagles; they will run and not grow weary, they will walk and not be faint.
— Isaiah 40:31

They say April showers bring the flowers in May
But I feel like I've been rained on for over a year straight
I've cried so many tears
That my eyes dried out
Wondering if God hears
The times that I cried out
Like, can you change my situation?
He said: Why? You're the one that needs changing
All you're focused on is the darkness and not my light

But when did I ever tell you you should walk by sight
That's never been how I operate
I never said it would be easy, still you said you would cooperate
But I promised I'd be with you in the midst of this
And I haven't left your side, not even for a little bit
You prayed for strength right? No one told ya?
The toughest battle gets fought by the strongest soldier
And when you need something to cry on you've always had my shoulder
Your biggest problem is you go about it like a loner
That's why I put some people in your life that I knew you need
And why I put some verses in your Bible that I knew you'd read
So you tell me. Were your prayers neglected?
Or was the answer just different than the one that you expected?

"Metamorphosis: Part 2," a spoken word poem by TEN20

BENNY "THE JET"

One day during college, some friends and I were tossing a football in the backyard at our house. I can't remember who, but somebody Knoblauched it. The football sailed over my head, over the neighbor's chain link fence, into their yard. We didn't know our neighbors at the time, but I figured it wouldn't be a big deal to hop over the fence, grab the ball, and proceed with our game of catch.

I carefully stuck one foot between the links, halfway up the fence, and threw my other leg over the top. Landing safely in the neighbor's yard, I made my way toward the pigskin. As I was reaching for it, it happened.

All I heard was a door shut and a dog bark. One of my favorite movies growing up was *The Sandlot*. All of the sudden, I was sure that I was Benny "The Jet" Rodriguez being pursued by The Beast. (If you haven't seen *The Sandlot*, you can put this book down and go watch it.)

With what my friends describe as sheer terror in my eyes, I grabbed the football, launched it back into our yard, and bolted for the fence. In my best attempt at a Jackie Chan type move, I aimed my hands for the top of the fence and pole-vaulted the rest of my body over it. To break the landing, I rolled three times through the dirty, poorly kept lawn. I arose, dirt stains on my clothes, sweat on my brow, breathing heavily. I had escaped. I turned back to make sure that The Beast was off my tail.

Right then, I knew I would never live down what had just happened. And I haven't. My friends laugh about it to this day, and I don't see that ceasing in this life or the next.

Two tiny wiener dogs, about a foot long each, weighing in at just under a combined 20 pounds, raced toward the fence, making little, high-pitched barking/squealing noises.

They had seen God send plagues on the Egyptians, split the Red Sea, send bread from heaven and water from a rock, accompany them in the form of a cloud by day and a pillar of fire by night, and much more. They should have trusted in His miraculous power and known that He would do what He said He would do!

I'm never going to live that one down.

This story reminds me of the Israelites, God's people, in the Old Testament of the Bible, when it was finally time to enter the Promised Land. I'll give you a brief summary, but I highly recommend reading it for yourself!

God had promised that He would give over the land of Canaan to His people, the Israelites. At this point, they should have been confident in God. They had seen God send plagues on the Egyptians, split the Red Sea, send bread from heaven and water from a rock, accompany them in the form of a cloud by day and a pillar of fire by night, and much more. They should have trusted in His miraculous power and known that He would do what He said He would do!

> The Lord said to Moses, "Send some men to explore the land of Canaan, which I am giving to the Israelites. From each ancestral tribe send one of its leaders" (Numbers 13:1–2).

God sends spies to check out the land. Why? He already said He was going to give the land to the Israelites. So why spy it out?

It seems to me that God was testing them. He knew they would see fortified cities and giants. He knew the spies would see, from a worldly perspective, that they had no chance. Would they trust God to do what He said He would do, even when it seemed impossible?

Ten out of twelve failed the test.

Only two spies, Joshua and Caleb, trusted God and urged the Israelites to take possession of the land. The rest were terrified. Their fear spread through the Israelites like cancer in the body.

As a result, Joshua and Caleb were the only two spies who lived to enter the Promised Land. The rest of the spies fell dead, and the entire generation that took on their fear-complex died in the wilderness over the next 40 years, never entering.

Had I seen from a higher perspective, I would not have fled for my life from two-foot-long wiener dogs. I would have seen I had nothing to fear.

Had the Israelites seen from God's perspective, they too would have had nothing to fear. The giants may have looked strong. The city walls may have seemed well fortified. But what is a giant to God? What wall could hold back the One who created the universe by His very word?

Instead, they accepted the bad report. The human way of seeing. The earthly perspective. And thus, they suffered the consequences.

Have you read the book *Unbroken* by Laura Hillenbrand? If not, you need to. In fact, put this book down and start reading *Unbroken*. Actually, just make *Unbroken* the next book you read after this one. It is, as the subtitle says, *A World War II Story of Survival, Resilience, and Redemption.*

At one point in the true story, Louis Zamparini and his two comrades had been lost at sea for several weeks. A Japanese plane flew over their life raft and fired its machine guns at the three castaway soldiers. Louis ducked for cover in the water, under the raft. Unfortunately, these were shark infested waters, and the sharks were hungry.

Put yourself in that situation. Lost at sea. Starving. Dying of thirst. Sun burned. Nothing in view besides the endless ocean. For a second, you think a plane is coming to rescue you. Instead, it fires bullets at you. As if being lost at sea isn't bad enough, now there are machine guns from above and sharks from below. Both attacking. Both trying to end the lives of you and your two fellow airmen.

It would have been easy to give up hope.

And of the three young airmen, one did.

The three men miraculously survive the attack and continue their journey, lost at sea. (Read *Unbroken* and you will better understand what I mean.) But Of the three, Louis, Phil, and Mac, only Louis and Phil hung onto hope. They talked of what life would be like after the war. They spoke of their loved ones. Their dreams and aspirations. They kept seeing a future for themselves.

Mac, on the other hand, withdrew. He lost the will to live.

And, he lost his life.

The three men had the same exact external circumstances. Same heat. Same starvation. Same thirst. Their difference was internal. It was perspective. It was will. It was hope.

I never want to minimize anyone's difficult circumstances. Everyone goes through difficult times. Some more than others. I am not here to minimize or to tell you just to snap out of it. I know firsthand it's not that easy.

I also know firsthand the power of hope.

Don't let your circumstances overpower you. Don't stop seeing a future for yourself. Don't lose the will to live.

Don't be like Mac.

Put a comma...

> *"I have told you these things, so that in me you may have peace. In this world you will have trouble. But take heart! I have overcome the world"* (John 16:33).

COMMA

A comma can change everything. Take these two sentences about three things I love: I love eating, my wife, and my son. *Or:* I love eating my wife and my son. One simple comma can transform the entire story! I once heard it said, don't put a period where God wants to put a comma.

We will all face many trials in this life. Some people choose to literally end their life while some do so in a figurative sense. They give up hope. They give up their dreams. Their spirit dies, and they wait around for their body to die too. Don't put a period at the end of your trial; put a comma. My FA diagnosis could have been my life's period. It could have ended the story. No more ministry, music, speaking, writing. No more hope. No more love.

I was determined to put a comma. I was determined to keep on fighting.

CAMPING PANCAKES

For a few consecutive summers in my early teens, my dad, brother, a few other men and I went on camping and canoeing trips in the wilderness. This was serious camping. On a scale of 1–10—1 being putting a tent up in the backyard and 10 being Man vs. Wild with Bear Grylls—our trips felt like about an 8. We would depart into the state park with nothing but backpacks, canoes, and paddles. We would canoe to a spot of land and then portage to a campsite. We'd set up our tents and cook over the fire. At night we would play cards and tell stories. The next day, we would wake up, make breakfast, pack up, and do it all over again.

> My FA diagnosis could have been my life's period. It could have ended the story. No more ministry, music, speaking, writing. No more hope. No more love.

When we reminisce about these trips, we always talk about how we had the best meals. In reality, the meals were pretty average. Pancakes, sandwiches, hot dogs, nothing we hadn't had before. But after spending all day paddling a canoe and then carrying it on your back, you get hungry. You aren't sitting on the couch and going to the fridge to snack all day. When it's finally time to eat, that pancake—which is no different than the pancakes you have eaten before—is the best thing you have ever tasted.

When you're hungry, food tastes better. When you are hot and thirsty, a cold drink tastes better than when you are well hydrated and at normal temperature.

I was hungry and thirsty for hope.

For inspiration.

Some days, it took everything in me just to get out of bed. I forced myself to get up, get dressed, brush my teeth, go to the gym, and go to work. I wore a smile on my face. I continued to minister and share messages about Jesus. Inside, everything was crumbling. I was wrestling with God. I wondered if He loved me. *Why would He allow me to be in this situation? Why did so many Christians pray for me and nothing happened? Why didn't going to church, praying, or reading the Bible make me feel any better?*

I was going through the motions. I went to the gym, to work, to church, to social gatherings, to family dinners, but my heart didn't go with me. I have great friends and family members, but I still felt I had no one to talk to. *Who could relate to my situation?* I thought about going to therapy, *but what could a therapist tell me about having FA?* I didn't even want to share my feelings with Abigail. I knew she was struggling with my diagnosis, and I didn't want to burden her even more with my issues.

For years I had been preaching about having an eternal perspective. I had written songs and poems and given messages about having hope in Jesus and persevering through trials. Now it was time to show that I really believed everything I had been saying.

I felt lost.

On one of the many days, I felt this way—it's really all a blur—a memory popped into my head. The memory was of one of our Real Men Bible study nights years earlier. One night after eating, Wayne gathered all the guys in front of the TV to watch a video. The video was of a man named Inquoris "Inky" Johnson sharing his story. Inky grew up with 14 people in a two-bedroom home and decided as a young boy that he was going to play in the NFL. He worked his whole life to make it to the NFL, and his dream was on the edge of becoming a reality. He had played so well as a sophomore in college that had he another good season, he was projected to be a first round draft pick. In only the second game of his junior season, a routine tackle landed him in a life-saving emergency surgery. Though his life was spared, the injury left him with a paralyzed arm, which ended his football career. Everything he had worked for his whole life was all over in the blink of an eye.

I remembered watching this video on that Thursday night years earlier and feeling inspired. I pulled up YouTube on my phone and typed "Inky Johnson" in the search bar. This same video popped up as the first result. I clicked on it, not knowing that my entire perspective on my situation was about to transform.

This video was like those camping trip meals. I remembered the video being good the first time I watched it. This time, it was the best video I had ever seen. This time, I felt a connection with Inky's story that I didn't have before. At one point in the video, he points out that when bad things happen, most people ask, "Why me?" He says, "Why not me?" A trial of this magnitude was the perfect opportunity for him to show what it truly means to persevere and, in doing so, be a blessing to others. He explains that when life gives people an opportunity to quit, most people take it because they don't have a driving force that is bigger than themselves.

I believe that God led me to this video because it was exactly what I needed to hear at that moment. For years I had been preaching about having an eternal perspective. I had written songs and poems and given messages about having hope in Jesus and persevering through trials.

Now it was time to show that I really believed everything I had been saying. I had also said I wanted my life to testify to God's glory. Well, now I had my chance. *In what better way could I glorify God than to persevere by faith in the face of being diagnosed with FA?*

> *I consider that our present sufferings are not worth comparing with the glory that will be revealed in us* (Romans 8:18).

REAL LIFE

When my perspective began to change, I began to see God move right away. Part of my job with Young Life consisted of serving at camp for four weeks during the summer. Each week, a new group of 500+ teens would come to camp ready to experience the best week of their lives. My job that summer was to be a "head leader," which sounds more fancy than it really is.

One of the head leader's roles is to walk around to each cabin at night and make sure every teen is accounted for. I would knock on the door and ask the cabin leader if everyone was present. For some cabins, it was that simple; for others, they would ask questions, wanting me to stay and talk or to rap for them—somehow, word got around camp that I was a hip-hop artist.

Part of the camp program includes sessions called Real Life. During Real Life, 4–5 adults share their faith stories with the 500+ teens over a span of four days. I was one of the adults selected to share.

One week, a group from Lincoln, Nebraska, came to camp. I felt a connection with this group due to my family history. My dad is from Lincoln, and several of my family members were Cornhuskers. For several years growing up, we went to Lincoln each year for Thanksgiving, went to a Husker football game, and even ate red hot dogs—all true Husker fans know exactly what I'm talking about.

As I got to know the group from Lincoln, I found out the University of Nebraska was recruiting one of their guys to play quarterback. During Real Life, I shared my story and talked about the emptiness I felt when I had put my identity into athletics and popularity versus the fulfillment I had found when I put my identity in being a child of God. I talked about my diagnosis and how I had put my hope in eternity and not in my physical body.

At the end of the week, before getting on the bus to go home, the young man who was a future Division 1 quarterback came up to me and gave me a hug. He thanked me for sharing my story, and I could tell he was fighting back tears.

At that moment, I realized that my story was bigger than I am.

My story had touched this young man.

My story was meant to touch others.

I realized that, in all my suffering, God had a purpose.

> Not only so, but we also glory in our sufferings, because we know that suffering produces perseverance; perseverance, character; and character, hope. And hope does not put us to shame, because God's love has been poured out into our hearts through the Holy Spirit, who has been given to us (Romans 5:3–5).

CHAPTER 17

MICHAEL JORDAN

And we know that in all things God works for the good of those who love
him, who have been called according to his purpose.
— Romans 8:28

I know God has a purpose
If it wasn't for my trials, I never would've written these verses
And if everything in my life was perfect
Then, really I would have no reason to worship
Cuz you don't know what healing is til you've had a broken heart
And the light shines brighter when you come out of the dark
And all my doubts just made my faith unshakable
And all my pain made my spirit unbreakable
See my story is something only God could write

I would have never known my purpose if I never had to fight this fight

And there's a reason I've endured all those sleepless nights

So I could tell you that everything is gonna be alright

Cuz heaven is my home and this earth is only temporary

So you don't have to cry when you lay me in the cemetery

And I can say that truthfully

Cuz I'll know I stood for something on the day they read my eulogy

One of God's soldiers you can bet I'm on the roster

And, no weapon formed against me shall prosper

So I'll press on, whatever storm I may weather

Cuz for those who love God, all things work together

"Metamorphosis: Part 3," a spoken word poem by TEN20

https://www.ten20words.com/metamorphosis

CHIPOTLE AND PIANO

One of my best friends, Alex, has always been a bit of a schemer. I've sometimes been part of his schemes, either willingly or unwillingly. In fact, he actually schemed up the first date that Abigail and I ever went on, which I partook in willingly. We once climbed up the rafters of our University's auditorium. I'm deathly afraid of heights but, somehow, Alex got me on board. Another time, when coaching a high school baseball team together, the school bus failed to pick our team up for practice. Alex gave me a devious look and next thing I knew, we had 11 teenage boys and their equipment sardine piled on top of one another in the back two-thirds of my minivan. My heart raced as we drove past a police car that either didn't see us or didn't want to deal with the situation—I now regret that stunt and have matured so much since that I would never do such a thing again! Furthermore, Alex and I delivered a memorable series of skits at Young Life club in character as Dingo Dave and Outback Willie. This just begins the list of our shenanigans.

All that said, on one occasion, I should have picked up on the fact that Alex was scheming. I didn't.

It was after dinner in the dining center. Probably Swedish meatballs. So, in other words, cereal for me because I have gone nowhere near Swedish meatballs since they taught me what explosive diarrhea is.

Alex and I were set to ride back to our college house together. This was the semester I had been taking the beginning piano class, and I had planned to go to the piano rooms after dinner for a short practice session. Alex convinced me to shoot hoops instead, assuring me that I could play the piano when we were done.

> Alex gave me a devious look and next thing I knew, we had 11 teenage boys and their equipment sardine piled on top of one another in the back two-thirds of my minivan.

After we took on two of the stars on the actual varsity basketball team in a riveting—for us, not them—game of two-on-two, we retired from the court that night. Alex decided it was too late for my piano practice and that we should head home. I reminded him of his earlier promise that I could tickle the ivories after we shot buckets.

"You can play on the keyboard at home," said Alex as if it were a well-known fact we had a keyboard sitting at the Clubhouse. I should have known right then.

He told me it was in "Phil's closet" in the basement. I assured him that he was wrong. I had just been in that closet the night before. No keyboard. Had there been a keyboard in our house, I would have been the first to know. I was the only one who could play it—sort of—and was currently obsessed with piano. I would have been playing it constantly. I would have loved if there had been a keyboard at the Clubhouse! I would have been thrilled! But I knew it was too good to be true. I knew Alex was wrong.

I was so confident, in fact, that I took on Alex's wager: three Chipotle burritos. When I went to Chipotle as a hungry college kid, I would order a bowl with two tortillas and a double order of everything besides meat—no extra charge! Then, I would make two burritos. So really, I was confident enough to bet six Chipotle burritos, a very high wager for a college student.

We shook hands and were off to the Clubhouse...after a quick bathroom break that I didn't think twice about in the moment. Alex opened the Club-house door with the same look on his face that he gave me before we broke every law for baseball team transportation.

As I walked down the stairs and opened the closet doors, I couldn't believe my eyes. There in front of me was all my dreams come true. A keyboard. I could now practice the piano in the comfort of my own home. I could even plug in headphones, so I didn't bother my roommates with the noise or incorrect notes. My excitement outweighed my disappointment over the six-burrito-sized hole that had just burned through my pocket.

God has great plans for us. He has all things at His disposal, and He is ready to shower blessings on His children. When we align our hearts with His heart, He delights in granting our deepest desires.

I was dumbfounded. How had I missed the keyboard in the closet this whole time?

I hadn't.

When the keyboard was gone a few days and six Chipotle burritos later, the truth came out. Alex's alleged bathroom break was really a business call. He had told our other roommate, Toedter—pronounced like tater-tot hotdish for all my Minnesotans—that if he could have a keyboard in Phil's closet in the next fifteen minutes, a Chipotle burrito (or two) awaited him.

They got me good.

Believe it or not, this story does have a moral. Alex showed me something about God, and how we too often approach—or fail to approach—Him. I so badly wanted a keyboard to be in that closet. But I knew there wasn't. I knew it was too good to be true. So much so, I made the largest wager of my life in my disbelief. But Alex, like God, is a person of schemes. The main difference being that God isn't trying to trick us into buying Him lunch and dinner for the weekend.

God has great plans for us. He has all things at His disposal, and He is ready to shower blessings on His children. When we align our hearts with His heart, He delights in granting our deepest desires.

> *"If you, then, though you are evil, know how to give good gifts to your children, how much more will your Father in heaven give good gifts to those who ask him"* (Matthew 7:11)!

> *"Delight yourself in the Lord,*
> *and he will give you the desires of your heart"* (Psalm 37:4).

All too often, we don't believe it. We stay away from God. We fail to align our hearts with His, and thus believe that He doesn't want to give us our heart's desires.

We even bet against God. We bet our time. Our paychecks. Our hopes. Our dreams. Our plans. Our security. Our careers. All against God. Against the One who made us. Who loves us. Who died for us. Who offers us new life.

Don't bet against God.
You're going to lose.
Just like I lost six burritos.
Take Him at His word.

BENEATH THE SURFACE

Living with FA, I've had to accept the fact that I will often be misperceived. I was once pulled over for rolling through a stop sign. The officer made me get out of the car and do multiple sobriety tests, which I failed. He called in backup before I could convince him just to give me the breathalyzer. Due to my bad balance, people have assumed I am drunk or just uncoordinated. Due to my slow, slurred speech, people tend to think I abuse drugs or am intellectually challenged.

The issue is that people only see the symptoms; they don't see the underlying cause. It is easy to see I have bad balance and that my speech is somewhat impeded; what's not easy to see is that I have a genetic irregularity causing these symptoms. I was born with this genetic complication, and there is nothing I can do on my own to fix it. I can exercise and do physical therapy to improve slightly, but I can't fix the underlying issue.

There is a difference between *sins* and *sin*. *Sins* are easy to identify; they are evident in plain sight. Murder, gossip, theft, adultery, envy, selfishness, and so on. However, *sins* are just the symptoms of the sickness that lies beneath the surface: *sin*. *Sin* is the condition of the human heart that is separated from God. *Sin* comes down to the desire to be the gods of our own lives—to have our own autonomy, seek fulfillment on our own, and go our own way, apart from God.

> *We all, like sheep, have gone astray,*
> *each of us has turned to our own way;*
> *and the Lord has laid on him*
> *the iniquity of us all* (Isaiah 53:6).

Sin manifests itself with many symptoms, and it is the reason our world is so broken today. We can alleviate some of the symptoms on our own. We can try to be more kind, less selfish, and to do good in the world. On our own, though, we can do nothing to correct the brokenness in our hearts.

I hope that FA is someday cured, especially in my lifetime. I recognize, though, that FA is not my biggest problem. FA can only affect me in this life; sin can separate me from my purpose, my Creator, and from all that is good—for eternity. My greatest issue has been solved. My biggest question has been answered. My deadliest disease has been cured. God's love and forgiveness have healed my broken heart.

How about you?
How is your heart?
Your soul?
Will you keep going your own way?
Will you keep seeking true fulfillment?
Will you keep believing the lie that if you accumulate enough possessions or achieve enough success that you will finally be satisfied?
That you will finally be happy?

Jesus stands at the door of your heart and knocks. He is knocking now as you read these very words. Don't spend another day with the door shut. Don't spend another day disconnected from who you were meant to be.

Open the door.

There is something great waiting on the other side.

> *Here I am! I stand at the door and knock. If anyone hears my voice and opens the door, I will come in and eat with that person, and they with me* (Revelation 3:20).

THE LAST DANCE

ESPN ingeniously released a documentary about Michael Jordan and the Chicago Bulls called *The Last Dance* in April of 2020, during the heart of the Covid-19 lockdown. Basically, all professional and college sports were shut down, so *The Last Dance* was the only thing sports fans had to watch! There is a moment in the documentary that shows Michael Jordan hugging the NBA Championship Trophy for the first time. This is an iconic moment in sports history, and any basketball fan can see this picture in their head. Watching *The Last Dance* gave me an even greater appreciation for this moment.

I hope that FA is someday cured, especially in my lifetime. I recognize, though, that FA is not my biggest problem. FA can only affect me in this life; sin can separate me from my purpose, my Creator, and from all that is good—for eternity.

It took years of hard work, years of losses, failures, and crushed dreams, and years of continuously overcoming to get to that moment. I have always had a love for these types of moments. The moments when hard work pays off. The moments when all the pain, blood, sweat, and tears are all worth it. There is something special about the tears streaming down the face of the young man who has worked his entire life to make it and has just been drafted to the NFL. In many cases, these moments may be attached to a championship or a big paycheck. Mine was not.

Over and Over Again

When someone decides to get into shape physically, that initial decision is the easy part. But the decision doesn't get the job done. It needs to be made again and again, multiple times each day. When you're tired and don't want to work out, you need to decide again. When you're hungry and would rather eat a bag of chips than a salad, you need to decide again.

Sometimes, you will fail. Eventually, though, if you stick it out, you will meet your goals. This illustrates how it was for me to make a change in my perspective. Deciding to embrace the situation and make the most of it is just the starting point. The decision needs to be made again and again, day in and day out.

> When my perspective changed, FA didn't. I still deal with the same realities. I still wonder how I am going to play with my kids or dance with my wife. I still fear losing my ability to walk and speak clearly.

When my perspective changed, FA didn't. I still deal with the same realities. I still wonder how I am going to play with my kids or dance with my wife. I still fear losing my ability to walk and speak clearly. I still fight the assumptions that I am an alcoholic or not intelligent. I still have to deal with the humility of the things that "the man should do"—like carrying the heavy stuff to the car—falling on my wife instead of me. I still have to deal with the stares and the stairs. No pun intended, but both stares and stairs can be difficult to deal with! Not every day or every moment is easy or perfect; in fact, it is quite the opposite.

Pressure Makes Diamonds

My wife would tell you that I am not the best at expressing my emotions. And she's right. It can be hard to be vulnerable when you are the leader of a ministry and a coach. It feels like so many people look up to you that you have to be strong, even if you don't feel like it. The best way I knew how to express my emotions was by writing them into songs.

This was a healing experience for me. Not only was I able to express myself; I was able to do so in a way that could help others. I poured the story of my diagnosis, and all of the emotions that came along with it, into a hip-hop album called *Pressure Makes Diamonds*. The featured song of the album says *pressure makes diamonds and fire makes gold*.

1 Peter 1:7 explains that in the same way that fire is used to refine and purify gold, trials in our lives are meant to purify and strengthen our faith. It is extreme pressure and heat that make the most beautiful, valuable stones on earth. In the same way, the trials we go through can shape us into a strong person with unshakeable faith if we let them.

SCAN OR VISIT

https://album.link/wHM2QTvVCtbx0

Pressure Makes Diamonds was the beginning of me taking my art in a different direction. One day, I was complaining about how I didn't have the funds or resources that I needed to make my career as a speaker and spoken word/ hip-hop artist take off. My dad gave his unsolicited opinion that I was aiming my art at the wrong crowd.

I had always loved Christian hip-hop, so I naturally aimed my music and poetry toward the CHH community. My dad suggested instead that I share my art with the rare disease, and specifically, the Ataxia community, as those were the people who would resonate more closely with my situation. At first I thought he was wrong and didn't know anything about the music industry. After thinking more about it, though, I thought maybe he was onto something. The least I could do was give it a try.

MY TROPHY

I was part of a few Facebook groups within the Ataxia community, and I shared one of my videos with these groups—the video was an unprofessional music video shot with my iPhone of me holding my cane and rapping a verse. The next day, I was shocked. Overnight, the video went from 300 to 1,500 views and had an overwhelming number of comments—compared to the rest of my stuff, not compared to Beyonce. As usual, my dad was right. I realized that music and poetry could allow me to speak hope and encouragement and share God's love with people who are in a situation just like I am.

As I continued sharing more content within the Ataxia community, the response was amazing. There were countless comments and messages from different people who had been touched and inspired by music and/or other videos. Among one of those messages was someone asking for my address; he wanted to send me one of the shirts he and his wife had made for their 11-year-old son, Boston, who also has FA. I am always hesitant to give out my address on the internet, but this seemed legitimate, so I decided to do it.

Weeks later, after I had pretty much forgotten about the message, my Jordan moment came. There was no trophy. No contract. No million-dollar check. There was, however, proof that all my hard work had paid off. Proof that my pain wasn't worthless. I held in my hand the very thing that drives me to persevere, the ability to impact someone just like me. I held a T-shirt that read "BOSTON STRONG" on the front, Isaiah 41:10 on the back, and handwritten note. *(See photo on next page.)*

> This note may not seem like much on the surface. It may not be a shiny trophy or one million dollars. Still, it meant the world to me. This note is the reason I get out of bed every day.

This note may not seem like much on the surface. It may not be a shiny trophy or one million dollars. Still, it meant the world to me. This note is the reason I get out of bed every day. Boston messaged me, telling me that he loved my music, and thanking me for speaking encouraging words. I wasn't (very) noticeably impacted by FA until my twenties. I can't imagine what it would be like expressing symptoms as young as Boston. If I think my situation is difficult, it is nothing compared to what Boston has to deal with. The fact that my music, poetry, speaking, and hopefully, this book, could impact someone like Boston means that all the pain I have experienced is worth it.

If by my perseverance through suffering, someone else can be encouraged and inspired to persevere in their situation, then my suffering is not in vain. When I get down, I think of all the Bostons out there. All the people whom life has dealt a difficult hand. I think of the fact that I could impact one soul. That I could help one person find the strength to persevere. That I could help one person find their purpose. That I could help one person see the love of the Father. Then, I am determined to press on.

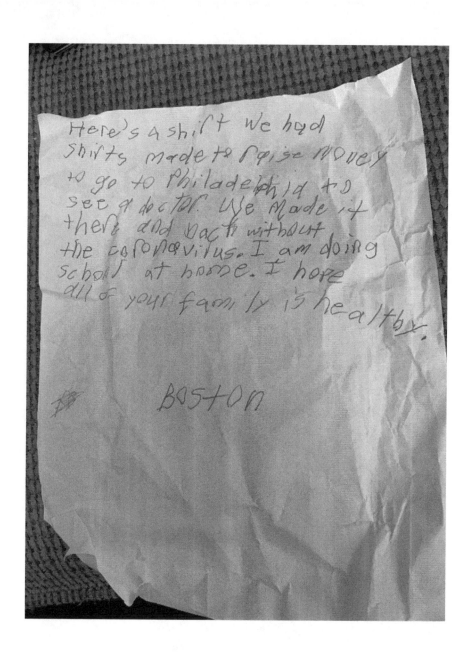

Here's a shirt we had shirts made to raise money to go to Philadelphia to see a doctor. We made it there and back without the coronavirus. I am doing school at home. I hope all of your family is healthy.

BOSTON

CHAPTER 18

COMMIT TO LIVE

You intended to harm me, but God intended it for good to accomplish what is now being done, the saving of many lives.

— Genesis 50:20

Rare disease, it really isn't that rare
Maybe you have one and feel like life isn't fair
Maybe you feel like you're all on your own
I know I've felt like I'm all alone
But the truth is, 1 in 10 are affected
Most cases are genetic, while some are caused by infections
Over 30 million in the US, 7,000 different diseases
Most have no funding, no research, no treatments
Friedreich's Ataxia, that's my condition

I had dreams of playing sports at high level competition
Then rare disease came and knocked me off track
But I won't be defeated, no instead I fight back
And you can fight with me, yeah you could have an impact
Maybe you have a lot and wonder how you can give back
You could fund the research that could cure one of us
Or maybe you're just a friend, could lend an ear to one of us
You could raise awareness
One click you could share this
You could be the answer to so many people's prayer list
If we work together, there's no impossible task
Odds are you know someone, all you gotta do is ask
But maybe you're that someone with the rare diagnosis
And maybe like me, at times you feel hopeless
But don't keep it in, so many people care for you
And when you feel like no one's there, God is always there for you
So don't give up, you might be close to a breakthrough
And your trials aren't meant to break you, but to make you
So as long as I can I'll keep on writing
And while you got breath in your lungs, keep on fighting.

"Keep On Fighting," a spoken word poem by TEN20

https://www.youtube.com/watch?v=KSpGdpOOmKA&t=1s

Broccoli and Boogers

I need to make a confession. I pick my nose. Not in public, that's just gross. But when I'm home alone, and there is gold to be dug, I dig. Abigail looks at me with disgust when she vacuums behind the coach. My sister, Kristin, once unleashed an all-out, two-armed, Ip Man-type attack on me when I misfired a booger flick, landing it on her and distracting her from a Law & Order SVU rerun episode.

This is unattractive, I know. But, I can proudly say I never got into eating my boogers. That is really gross—to all my booger eaters out there, you should get help.

I'll never forget a joke told by my high school friend, Matt. The reason this joke was so memorable is that it was told when Matt was about 4 years old. Other friends and I got to see it performed when his family was playing old home videos one night.

> When you create something, you know how it works and what it needs. God created us. He knows exactly what we need, which is often different from what we want.

"What's the difference between broccoli and boogers?" 4-year-old Matt inquired.

"What?" the camera man responded.

"Kids don't eat broccoli."

I'm laughing just thinking about it. The punch line gets me every time.

My son, Titus, recently miracle-grew tall enough to reach onto the counter-tops. He wants everything he shouldn't have. With a room full of colorful, noise-making toys, he still wants the remote. When you take away something he wants, something that is harmful to him—think serrated knife or full glass of wine—he becomes distraught. He weeps as if the world were ending.

At some point, he will be old enough to make his own decisions. We will raise him to the best of our abilities. But someday, he will do what he wants with his life.

Kids don't choose broccoli. They want candy. Walk through the cereal aisle at the grocery store. You will see that Cap'n Crunch, Fruity Pebbles, and Count Chocula are on the bottom row, at eye-level and within reach of small children. Grape Nuts, Kashi, and Fiber One occupy the higher rows, tempting my mother, knowing the complaints that await her at home if she gives in and buys them. Grocery stores know exactly what they're doing.

Children don't know what they need. They don't know what is best for themselves. They need a loving parent to lead and guide them. They need someone to discipline them, telling them they can't eat their dessert unless they finish their veggies—I still live by this principle, literally and figuratively. Thanks, mom and dad!

When you create something, you know how it works and what it needs. God created us. He knows exactly what we need, which is often different from what we want. When God lovingly and graciously says no, we turn into the temper-tantruming child, protesting in the cereal aisle as mom refuses to buy a box of Oreo O's cereal.

God is loving Father, but He won't force us to love Him in return. Forced love is no love at all. God wants us to *choose* to love Him. As I mentioned, someday, Titus will have to make his own decisions. It will break my heart if he makes choices that bring harm to himself or others. As badly as I may want to, I won't be able to control him.

God, in His grace, tells us no and draws guidelines for us. When we keep moving further and further away from Him, pursuing the desires of our sinful hearts, He will let us go. God won't turn His back on us, but He will watch, full of tears, as we turn our backs on Him. When we arrive at the destination that we so relentlessly pursue, we will realize just how empty it is. The success, the money, the acclaim. They always overpromise and underdeliver.

Remember in school when your teachers would say there's no such thing as a stupid question? We all knew that was a lie. The teacher was just trying to mitigate the bullying that awaited the kid who asked the dumb question. But now I'm wondering if my teachers were right. Twice in the Bible, Jesus asks what seems to me to be stupid questions. Knowing Jesus, though, I'm inclined to think I'm probably wrong about that.

Once, Jesus was walking down a busy street with His friends. Two blind men heard he was coming. Jesus's reputation often preceded Him. These blind men had likely heard of the miracles He had been doing, and thus, they shouted for Jesus. People shooshed them, probably putting one finger across their lips and making a *ssshhhh* sound. They didn't care. This was their chance. Jesus was walking by. They shouted and shouted for Him.

"What do you want me to do for you?" (Matthew 20:32);

Really, Jesus? That was your question? I can hear Mrs. Vulna, my 1st grade teacher, raising her voice above the snickers of the entire class, reminding them there is no such thing as a stupid question. A reminder much needed in this case.

So why did Jesus ask a question that seemed to have such an obvious answer? As I have pondered this story, I have come to a conclusion. Jesus saw the reality beyond the physical realm. He knew these men had a deeper need than the restoration of their sight. The eyes of their hearts needed to be opened to see Jesus for who He really was. The restoration of their physical eyes would surely help them in this life. The restoration of their spiritual eyes would help them for eternity. I believe that by asking this question, Jesus was trying to provoke these men, and everyone else, to think deeply about what they wanted Him to do for them.

What do you want Jesus to do for you? He told a paralyzed man to get up and walk. He gave sight to the blind, cleansed lepers, delivered demoniacs, and even raised the dead. Yes, these miracles helped people to live better lives, and that is important. But that wasn't the sole purpose of His works of wonders.

> *Knowing their thoughts, Jesus said, "Why do you entertain evil thoughts in your hearts? Which is easier: to say, 'Your sins are forgiven,' or to say, 'Get up and walk'? But I want you to know that the Son of Man has authority on earth to forgive sins." So he said to the paralyzed man, "Get up, take your mat and go home." Then the man got up and went home. When the crowd saw this, they were filled with awe; and they praised God, who had given such authority to man* (Matthew 9:4–8).

I have asked God to heal me from FA. We have probably all done something similar. We have asked God to heal our dying loved ones. To give us a promotion. To let us make the team. To get the prom date. When you don't have something, it's easy to think that thing will be fulfilling. When single or dating, you think marriage will fulfill you. When broke, you think money will fulfill you. When you are riding Metro Transit, you think a car will fulfill you. It won't. How do I know? History is full of examples of people who had everything and yet weren't fulfilled. We are the kid at the grocery store, reaching for the Cookie Crisp. God knows the occasional bowl of Reese's Puffs is fine to enjoy. But we also need broccoli.

Now that I'm an adult, I like broccoli—and now that I know how to properly roast it after dressing it with olive oil, salt, and pepper. As we get to know God more and more, we'll see that He has our best interests in mind. He is looking out for us. We will know how to answer when He asks us what we want Him to do for us.

Which brings me to the second seemingly stupid question from Jesus. Jesus approached a man who had been physically disabled for thirty-eight years. This was the best thing he could think to say—brace yourself: *"Do you want to get well"* (John 5:6)?

Seriously? This time even Mrs. Vulna chuckles. It seems like the perfect question for Captain Obvious. Until we hear the answer. Actually, it is less of an *answer* and more of a *response*. The man didn't actually answer the question. He just started making excuses. Meanwhile, the One with the power to heal him was standing right in front of him asking if he wanted to be healed! Imagine a patient with a critical wound explaining to the surgeon why his wound can't be repaired while the surgeon is standing there, tools in hand, ready to perform the operation.

> Maybe your struggle is obvious and physical like Friedreich's Ataxia. Maybe it's less obvious like childhood trauma or anxiety. Don't let your struggle become your identity. Don't let your struggle control you. Don't let it write your narrative.

Don't be too quick to laugh. This could be you. It could be me. We all have struggles. Some are more obvious and extreme than others, but we all have them. There is a temptation to make your struggle your identity. When this happens, people can easily slip far from their potential and their purpose, all the while making their struggle their excuse. Their struggle becomes everything. They are controlled by it. To the point that if Jesus stood before them and asked if they wanted to be healed, they wouldn't even answer the question. They would continue with their excuses.

Maybe your struggle is obvious and physical like Friedreich's Ataxia. Maybe it's less obvious like childhood trauma or anxiety. Don't let your struggle become your identity. Don't let your struggle control you. Don't let it write your narrative.

Seek God in your struggle. Find your identity in what He says about you. Let Him write your narrative.

Therefore we do not lose heart. Though outwardly we are wasting away, yet inwardly we are being renewed day by day (2 Corinthians 4:16).

V8 Splash and Poopy Diapers

I have written the bulk of this book during the COVID-19 pandemic. With everything being shut down, there isn't much else to do. A surefire sign in 2020 that someone has COVID-19 is the loss of taste and smell. Sure enough, I eventually contracted the virus. Since we weren't certain whether or not Abigail and Titus had been infected, I went to quarantine at my parents' house since they had already tested positive.

In general, I try to eat a pretty healthy diet. As mentioned before, though, I do have a bit of a sweet tooth. My sweet tooth comes out especially at my parents' house. I usually avoid sugary drinks completely, mainly to balance out my cookie intake. This particular morning at my parents', however, I wasn't feeling well, and as far as my typical health regimen was concerned, all bets were off. I put two mini cinnamon rolls in the microwave and poured myself a glass of V8 Splash (aka water + high fructose corn syrup).

> The good far outweighs the bad. This doesn't mean the *bad* is not real or insignificant. It just means the *good* is more good than the *bad* is bad.

My first sip was one of my life's greatest disappointments. It was early in the morning, and my brain wasn't functioning well enough yet to connect the dots. I checked the expiration date on the bottle—that wasn't the problem. The microwave dinged, and I got my cinnamon rolls out. With much anticipation, I took my first bite. Nothing. That's when it hit me. There was nothing wrong with the juice or rolls. My COVID-19 symptoms, the loss and taste and smell, had activated overnight.

Over the next month, I learned there was an upside not to be able to taste or smell. I could eat plain spinach without having to taste it. I couldn't smell Titus' poopy diapers. I didn't have to worry about who was in the bathroom before me. But when I began to weigh the pros and cons, it became obvious that not being able to taste and smell is worse than the flipside. There are so many amazing smells and tastes in this world. Homemade cookies, *carne asada* burritos, jerk chicken, and fried plantains. The aromas when you walk outside and know that spring has sprung or that the leaves will soon fall and it's time for football season. The good far outweighs the bad. This doesn't mean the *bad* is not real or insignificant. It just means the *good* is more good than the *bad* is bad.

Many people choose to live in a metaphorical state similar to the symptoms of COVID-19. They don't want to risk the pain of heartbreak, so they choose not to love. They don't want to risk the shame of failure, so they choose not to try. They don't want to risk disappointment, so they choose not to hope. Their souls are sick. Living with FA, the *bad* is very bad. I have had to learn to take the good along with the bad.

You may also have a difficult situation, but don't let your soul get sick.
Don't give up your joy.
Don't give up your hope.

GIVE IT TO GOD

To say that Joseph of the Bible had a rough go would be a major understatement. When he was just a boy, his brothers were jealous of him and sold him into slavery. He was then sold to a powerful man named Potiphar. Potiphar's wife was attracted to Joseph and tried time after time to seduce him. But Joseph, choosing to do the right thing, refused her. She then falsely accused Joseph of attempting to rape her, and Joseph was thrown in prison. While in prison, Joseph helped a man of high standing and asked that this man get him out of prison, but the man forgot about him. Joseph was wronged time and again, but he refused to turn away from God. He could have been mad at God for what his brothers did and used that as an excuse to give into temptation with Potiphar's wife. He didn't.

Eventually, Joseph became a ruler of Egypt. God warned him of a coming famine, and he stored grain ahead of time. Meanwhile, his brothers in Israel and the rest of God's people were running out of food. Joseph's brothers had to come and buy food from him just to survive. This could have been a perfect opportunity for Joseph to get revenge on his brothers. He could have refused to sell them food or even had them killed. Instead, Joseph saw that God was using the tragedies in his life for a bigger purpose. Joseph forgave his brothers and welcomed all of Israel to come live in Egypt. Joseph chose to pursue God's purpose rather than his own. In doing so, the lives of the Israelites were saved, and God's plan to redeem humanity was preserved.

This story is a perfect example of what can happen when we surrender ourselves to God's purpose. When I look back on my life, I see how God has been with me every step of the way. I see how God can even use something like my FA diagnosis for a bigger purpose. I used to want to be a professional athlete. My dream was all about myself. I wanted success, fame, money, and respect, all for myself.

I never planned to become a minister, a coach, an artist, an author, and a speaker. I don't believe God caused me to have FA; we live in a world that is broken and imperfect because of human sin. I do believe, however, God has used my FA diagnosis to guide me into His purpose for my life. God didn't cause Joseph's brothers to be filled with jealousy and commit the atrocity of selling him into slavery. However, God did use their decision to do so for a greater purpose. Whatever wrong you have suffered, God hasn't done it to you, but if you let Him, He will use it for good.

STICKS AND STONES

When I was 12, my family's two-week cabin trip fell smack dab in the middle of my all-star baseball season. This was the season I had dreamt about for years, ever since I had seen 12-year-olds playing in the Little League World Series on ESPN. Unfortunately, my Shoreview South All-Star team lost in the district playoffs and we weren't going to make it onto national television. So, off to the cabin we went.

My baseball season wasn't over, though, and we were scheduled for a tournament the weekend I had planned to get back. I would be missing several practices and didn't want to have a poor performance when I returned, so I came up with a plan. I found a nice stick in the woods that would serve as a perfect bat. Every day, I walked around with my makeshift bat for about an hour, finding stones to throw up in the air and hit with my "bat" as they came down.

When it came time for the tournament, I felt as prepared as ever. I caught wind later on, though, that not everyone had the same confidence in me after my two-week absence. My mom overheard another mom in the stands saying I had been gone for two weeks and may be rusty. For my first appearance at the plate, the bases were loaded. The pitcher threw one high and inside—my favorite. I swung and sent the ball over the outfielders. It hit halfway up on the fence, just a few feet away from a homerun. I was just getting warmed up. In my next at-bat, the bases were loaded again. I got another pitch I liked and sent it far over the fence for a grand slam. My team and our fans celebrated as I trotted the bases. It was great to be back.

Most people are at least somewhat familiar with the story of David and Goliath from the Bible. Goliath was a Philistine giant who openly insulted God and His people. Goliath challenged all of God's people and said that anyone could fight him one-on-one to settle the conflict between opposing armies. If Goliath won, God's people would become the Philistines' slaves. If Goliath's challenger won, the Philistines would be enslaved by God's people. No one dared accept his challenge until David came along.

David, a shepherd boy, the youngest of his brothers, caught wind of the situation. He couldn't believe the way Goliath was openly blaspheming God. David had confidence in God and knew, with God's help, he could defeat Goliath. David went to face Goliath with nothing but a sling. As Goliath was mocking David, David slung a perfect shot into Goliath's forehead. Then he cut off Goliath's head with his own sword. David saved the day and was a hero among God's people.

> I don't believe God caused me to have FA; we live in a world that is broken and imperfect because of human sin. I do believe, however, God has used my FA diagnosis to guide me into His purpose for my life.

Why was David so confident? What is less known about David is the fact that this fight with Goliath was not his first fight. David tended sheep. He was the only one out in the field. No one was watching. When a lion or bear came to steal a sheep, David would slay the animal with his sling and bring the sheep safely home. No one rewarded him. No one praised him. He was simply doing what he saw as his duty.

Everyone in the crowd saw me hit that grand slam when I was 12. What they didn't see was me practicing with sticks and stones every day leading up to that moment. Everyone saw David defeat Goliath. No one saw him defeat lions and bears in the remote fields.

I have had opportunities to speak and perform before thousands of people. I have been congratulated, applauded, and even paid. But before I was ever put on a stage or given a single penny, I was getting prepared. I have spent countless hours writing, recording, and rehearsing. I have poured my blood, sweat, tears, and finances into creating music and spoken word videos. Before I ever recorded, I traveled across the country for three weeks on the Megabus sharing spoken word poems with one or two guys at a time after playing pickup basketball. I never aspired to make money or get famous. I simply felt that God had given me a gift I was supposed to share. It is my duty.

Do you want to do something great in life? Do you want to defeat the giants you are facing? Don't start with Goliath. Start with the lion and the bear. Don't start in the batter's box in front of the crowd. Start with sticks and stones by yourself. David went on to be the greatest King in the history of God's people. He was the main author of the Book of Psalms—I like to think he was the spoken-word poet and hip-hop artist of his time. In the Psalms, we see that David had a deep relationship with God. He sought God out all by himself and poured out his heart to the Father.

> For some time, I thought having FA meant giving up on music, poetry, and ministry. Instead, I see that God has used and will continue to use a difficult circumstance to lead me into His plan for me.

Start there. Get alone with God. Pour your heart out to Him and allow Him to pour His heart out to you. Ask God who He wants you to be and what He wants you to do. Don't aspire toward money, fame, renown, or accomplishments. Aspire to know and be known by God, and you won't go wrong.

To Destiny

I wrote the poem that begins this chapter after finding out about a contest hosted by the National Institute of Health to raise awareness for rare diseases. I worked with a professional videographer to make the poem into a spoken word poetry video and submitted it to the judges. Sure enough, "Keep On Fighting" won first place!

The *Keep On Fighting* video was released to the world on several websites and media outlets, and the response from the rare disease community was overwhelming. I was asked to speak at the annual Rare Disease Day conference, appear on podcasts, write for blogs, and have received countless messages from people who were impacted by the video. For some time, I thought having FA meant giving up on music, poetry, and ministry. Instead, I see that God has used and will continue to use a difficult circumstance to lead me into His plan for me.

Living with FA, though it is challenging, provides me with a unique opportunity to inspire others to persevere and to put their faith in God. Jesus suffered. His suffering had a purpose. His death on the cross, followed by His resurrection, made a way for humanity to be reconciled to the Father. Looking at Jesus, I can see that suffering, when surrendered to God, is not in vain. My suffering has a purpose.

If I can keep faith through my circumstances. If I can persevere. If I can hold on to hope. Then I can help others to do the same. But, ultimately, I'm just a man. I make mistakes. If you put your hope and faith in me, I will disappoint you and fail you. Jesus won't. My true hope is that I can inspire you to put your hope in Him.

I also have a unique platform to raise awareness and resources to fight rare disease. As a speaker, author, and artist, I can use creative means to expose the reality of rare disease and the vast needs associated with the challenges that it brings. This can lead to more research and resources for those affected, myself included.

As I write this, I am currently scheduled to participate in a trial for a potential FA treatment. It would be amazing if a treatment and cure are found. I would love to be able to run again and play sports with my sons. But what if the study is unsuccessful? What if no treatment or cure comes out in my lifetime? Compared to eternity, this lifetime is short. I will spend eternity in a fully restored body in complete paradise; that reality can get me through each day with peace and joy in my heart.

THE YELLOW JIG

At the family cabin, there are typically two activities that—weather permitting or sometimes despite the weather—we do every day: tennis and fishing. For years of my childhood, I aspired to be a fishing guide someday—in retirement from the MLB of course. I was always rigging up everyone's line, impaling innocent leeches and minnows with rusty hooks, and taking fish off for the people who thought (knew) that touching fish is gross—after relentless hand washing with dish soap and regular hand soap, they still stink!

My dad had a couple of big tackle boxes in which the family would go hunting for jigs and Rapala lures that were in usable condition. I had my own tackle box. Extra line, needle nose pliers, scented rubber frogs that smelled like they had been aged in liquid dog food, the five variations of pocket knives that I purchased with my allowance. I had it all.

One summer, my most prized lure was the yellow jig. It was beautiful. Weighted perfectly. It danced through the water, attracting northern pike, largemouth bass, the occasional crappie or perch, and on a really lucky day, a walleye.

But one day in early June was not so lucky. I casted my yellow jig and recently deceased minnow across the drop off. *1, 2, 3, 4, 5, 6.* I knew exactly how many seconds to let the bait sink before reeling it just above the weeds. Reel, reel, reel, pull. The perfect technique—at least the one that works for me, in case a real pro fisherman reads this.

I felt what gets all fishermen excited: a fish. As custom, I slowly dragged my yellow jig, feeling the nibbles, and got ready to jerk my rod up, hooking the fish's lip—sorry to my PETA friends!

I jerked the rod, full of anticipation. My fisherman's heart quickly fell from cloud nine and landed on the boat floor, joining the segments of leftover line and fish scales that had accumulated over the years. Not only was the fish gone. It had made off with my yellow jig.

The story could have ended there.

It didn't.

Later that summer, we were back on the lake, hoping we could catch enough fish for dinner for about ten people who eat enough fish for twenty. I had moved on to a new lure and was jigging it along, when suddenly, I felt a fish take interest. Waiting for the perfect moment, I jerked and set the hook perfectly in the northern pike's lip. The fight was on. As usual and true to this day, I heard my dad in my head—and likely aloud—saying, "Keep your rod tip up!"

"Net!" I demanded as I wrestled the northern close enough to the boat for my sister to scoop up with the trusty fish net. As we pulled the pike aboard, I couldn't believe my eyes!

My yellow jig!

There it was, stuck in the northern's lip along with the new jig that had taken its place. I got the fish *and* my yellow jig—in due time.

Sometimes we set out with a big goal. We give it our all. And nothing happens. We lose the fish, and even our lure. We have less than we started with in the first place.

When I was 22 years old, newly married, and surviving on one ministry income while Abigail finished school, I spent my entire life savings to produce my first professionally recorded EP—like an album but shorter. My total piggy bank got me six songs—recording, production, mixing, and mastering—distribution on streaming platforms, and a professional music video. I guaranteed Abigail that this money would come back around. I was sure my video would blow up and get millions of views, leading to lots of paid shows and probably a million-dollar record deal.

It didn't. I didn't catch the fish. And I lost my jig in the process.

But I didn't give up.

I kept going. Kept adjusting. Kept adapting. Kept moving forward.

When I made the *Keep on Fighting* video and won first place, there was an award.

The award was the exact dollar amount of the life savings I had spent on my first EP.

> When I made the *Keep on Fighting* video and won first place, there was an award. The award was the exact dollar amount of the life savings I had spent on my first EP.

And the video reached and impacted thousands of people.

I got my fish back. And my yellow jig.

Five years later.

Things won't go as you planned. If they did, the story wouldn't be any fun. Imagine if Isildur had destroyed the ring of power right away. There would not have been any Lord of the Rings movies for me to watch every weekend from ages 10–15 (again, if you don't get it, put this book down and initiate a Lord of the Rings movie marathon!).

There are going to be bumps in the road. That is what makes the ride exciting.

Don't give up. Keep casting your line and finding new lures. In due time, you will catch your fish, and your yellow jig.

Keep on Fighting

Given modern technology, I could have been aborted. It could have been found out in my mother's womb that I would have FA. Doctors could have told my parents that life would be too hard, and it may be better to end it before it begins outside the womb.

Ask my friends and family. Ask the hundreds of teens I have coached and mentored. Ask the tens of thousands of people I have spoken to or the hundreds of thousands I have reached online.

Ask them if my life has been worth living.

It's not that I think I'm special. Everyone is special. The Bible says God has knit each one of us together in our mother's womb.

> *For you created my inmost being;*
> *you knit me together in my mother's womb* (Psalm 139:13).

Whoever you are, your life is worth living.
Don't give up hope.
Don't believe the lie that you are not significant.
Don't believe the lie that no one loves you or cares about you.
If you take nothing else from this book, I want you to make a commitment, right now, to live.
No matter what you are facing, live.
You matter.
Your life is worth it.
Keep on living.

Before being diagnosed with FA, I didn't have any major trials in my life. Of course, I had my fair share of disappointments, but I had not been through any extreme tragedies. One of the biggest things I realized through my diagnosis is that everyone has a story and will encounter significant trials in their life. Maybe you grew up in a broken home. Maybe you were abused. Maybe you have cancer or another health problem. Maybe you lost a loved one. The list goes on and on. Everyone has a challenge. Everyone has a reason to quit. Everyone has a reason to turn their back on God. Everyone has or will have the same decision to make. Will you turn from God and go your own way?

Will you give up on God's purpose for your life? Or, will you embrace your situation and allow God to work in you and through you?

Your story is not my story. Maybe you were abused, and God is going to use you to counsel and write books for people who are now coming up in the same situation. Maybe you grew up without a father, but God is going to use you as a father figure to other kids growing up without dads. Maybe you will die of cancer, and God will use your joy and hope as a testimony to those around you of the reality of an eternal hope in heaven.

Your story is not my story, but I wrote this book for you. I want you to know that God has a purpose for your life. I want you to know that no matter what you have gone through, what you're going through, and what you will go through, God has a plan for your life. If you surrender yourself to Him, you will find peace, joy, and hope in this life, and eternal paradise when it ends.

Everyone has a challenge. Everyone has a reason to quit. Everyone has a reason to turn their back on God. Everyone has or will have the same decision to make. Will you turn from God and go your own way? Will you give up on God's purpose for your life? Or, will you embrace your situation and allow God to work in you and through you?

No more pain. No more suffering. No more wrongdoing. No more tears. Who could say no to that? In everything you go through, always remember this: your trials aren't meant to break you; they're meant to make you!

Keep on fighting.

CLOSING THOUGHTS

But we have this treasure in jars of clay, to show that the surpassing power belongs to God and not to us.

— 2 Corinthians 4:7

I came to tell you, just don't give up now
And when you feel like, you've had enough now
You gotta trust now
That there's a purpose in your pain
Life ain't perfect, I'm just saying
There's always somehow
Or some way, that it could be worse
You still got hope, if you ain't in a hearse
Or a casket
Life threw me a curve
But "Why me?" is something I don't ask it
And yeah I've had some hard nights
But you could get dealt a bad hand, and still play your cards right
So I'm all in
Lord keep me from falling
I'm just tryna live out my calling
I used to have big dreams of ballin'
That I could be on TV
Where everyone could see me
Score a TD
But, thank God that He freed me
From my vain pursuits
I wanted fame and loot
'Til I met the one who took away my shame and guilt
Now when I get on the microphone I aim to kill

Every lie from the mouth of the serpent
Like, "You're worthless
And your life has no purpose
You should end it now"
I know some people feel that beneath the surface
So I'm bending down
To say a prayer for humanity
That we could get past our vanity
And treat others how we want them to treat us
Yeah, cuz that's the real way of Jesus
The more I look around, the more I see
God, only You could free us

"free us," a freestyle by TEN20

https://www.facebook.com/1081594375262750/videos/2746427208926876

I wrestled with whether or not to write this book. I felt the ending wasn't good enough; I wanted a perfect conclusion or resolution. I thought a better ending would entail the story of how I got a major record deal, how my music blew up, or how I became a world-renowned motivational speaker and top-selling author. I wanted to add the story of how I made millions of dollars and gathered millions of social media followers. With a title like *From Diagnosis To Destiny*, I felt the ending had to be truly special. I felt I had to be more successful than I am now.

But what is success?
Is it millions of dollars?

Millions of followers?
Millions of streams?

No.

The times I have felt most successful are not when my videos have gotten 50,000 views or after a good live performance. They are not when I've put a check in the bank.

I find success in the little things. The small moments.

When my wife, Abigail, says she is proud of me for the way I carry myself through my challenges.

When my eldest son, Titus, gives me a high five or when I catch my youngest son Griffin's eye and he smiles.

When my brother John told me my music had been positively impacting him.

When my niece Emma asked to interview me for a class project on facing adversity.

When I receive messages and comments from people or family members of people who are battling rare diseases.

I am going to keep making music. I am going to keep making spoken word poetry videos. I am going to keep speaking and writing. I am going to continue praying that all my creative efforts reach and impact the people whom they are meant for.

When I got a letter from Boston, Zoom called with George, flew out to stay with the Carrolls, or watched the NBA Finals with Corey.

To date, I am not famous and do not make much money as a speaker, author, and artist. And that is fine with me. I am going to keep making music. I am going to keep making spoken word poetry videos. I am going to keep speaking and writing. I am going to continue praying that all my creative efforts reach and impact the people whom they are meant for.

Money and fame will never define success for me. I now think the fact that I don't have much of either makes the ending of this book even better. Signing a major record deal may have been a great ending—and hey, I'm not opposed to that happening someday—but I feel it's much better to end here. Here in the struggle. There is no FDA-approved treatment for FA. I scrape by to pay the bills each month. I have many difficult days.

But …

I have a lot of joyful moments too. I have a beautiful family. I have a great community. Most of all, I have hope. I have faith in Jesus Christ. I have an eternal paradise awaiting me.

This is my destiny.

EPILOGUE

Now to him who is able to do immeasurably more than all we ask or imagine, according to his power that is at work within us, to him be glory in the church and in Christ Jesus throughout all generations, for ever and ever! Amen.

— Ephesians 3:20–21

I'm just checking in, reminding you to keep your head up
I know life can be hard, got you feeling fed up
The rain pours down, it won't even let up
Remember, it's not about how you fall, but how you get up
So when you're down don't stay too long
And, when your sad just play this song
And know your special and you got a purpose
God looks at you and He calls you worth it
Your people love and they care about you
And, this world wouldn't be the same without you
So, keep moving and keep shining
And when your under pressure, know that pressure makes diamonds

An excerpt from "1 OF A KIND.," a song by TEN20

https://song.link/i/1590152958

PANDEMIC

At the beginning of Chapter 8, I shared a poem called "The Cure." The poem describes a hypothetical scenario where everyone in the world has a deadly disease, but you have an infinite amount of the cure. What would you do? The poem then explains that this scenario is not hypothetical at all. Everyone in the world has a deadly disease: sin. If you are a follower of Jesus Christ, you have the cure. What are you going to do?

> COVID-19 can end your life on this earth. Sin can lead to eternal suffering and separation from your Creator, your purpose, and all that is good.

Though I released "The Cure" in 2015, it seemed more relevant than ever in 2020 when the global COVID-19 pandemic caused the world to shut down. While stuck at home, on March 12th, I decided to share "The Cure" on Facebook once again. My caption read: "This pandemic is making me think of the fact that we have a much deadlier disease than the coronavirus, but there is a CURE!" I don't at all say this to minimize the gravity of the pandemic. COVID-19 is extremely serious and has had devastating effects all around the world.

But sin is more serious.

COVID-19 can end your life on this earth.

Sin can lead to eternal suffering and separation from your Creator, your purpose, and all that is good.

> *Do not be afraid of those who kill the body but cannot kill the soul. Rather, be afraid of the One who can destroy both soul and body in hell* (Matthew 10:28).

1 OF A KIND.

Anyway, I never could have guessed what hitting that share button would lead to. I noticed in my notifications that someone had reposted "The Cure" with a caption that read something like: "A Christian with Friedreich's Ataxia, I finally found a rapper I can listen to." I thanked Clover Carroll for sharing the post, which led us into a conversation over Facebook Messenger and eventually a Zoom call. I came to find out that Clover and his wife Rachel have a son named Cooper who also has Friedreich's Ataxia. They are also creatives, entrepreneurs, and followers of Jesus. We had a lot to connect on!

We put our heads together over a few Zoom calls on how we could combine our efforts to fight rare disease and share the hope of Jesus in the process. We had a few ideas, but nothing concrete transpired.

Until one day… I had an idea!

Clover and Rachel run a media production and marketing company called New Story Media. They put their talents to work and created a fantastic video with their son, Cooper, to raise funds for FA research. This video has now raised more than $1,000,000 for research!

https://www.youtube.com/watch?v=deAQPqJOnF8

I had written a song called "1 OF A KIND." and had been thinking about making it into a music video. I pondered what would be the perfect storyline for the video.

And that's when it hit me.

The video with Cooper would be a perfect fit for my music video. I texted Clover to set up yet another Zoom call. I shared my grand idea with him and asked if he would let me use their video for my music video.

Clover did me one better.

He suggested that I fly down to Texas, stay with the Carroll family for a few days, and he would shoot and edit the video free of charge. A few weeks later, I was on a flight to the Lone Star State.

I had an amazing time getting to know the Carroll family and shooting the video. The video turned out great (in my humble opinion)! We released the song, video, and the 1 OF A KIND. shirt line on October 20th, 2021. The shirts are pretty cool (again, in my humble opinion) and every shirt purchase sends $1 to research for rare disease treatments. Follow the QR code below to see the video and the shirts!

https://www.ten20words.com/1ofakind

THANK YOU

If you are still reading, I just want to take a moment and say thank you. Truly, from the bottom of my heart, thank you. It means the world to me that you would take time to join me on the journey *From Diagnosis To Destiny*. I hope this can be the beginning of our journey together. I would love to come to your (or your kids') school, church, or wherever else people gather. Please don't hesitate to reach out to me! But, more importantly, I want to know your story. I want to know how this book has impacted you. I want to walk together on the path of our destinies. Follow the QR code below to join the "From Diagnosis to Destiny" Facebook group with me. Post a comment and share your story and what you have gained from reading this book. I look forward to connecting!

https://www.facebook.com/groups/593135438792001

Follow Jacob "TEN20" Thompson:

- **Website:** https://www.ten20words.com/
- **Instagram and Facebook**: @ten20words
- **YouTube** and all music platforms: TEN20